UNDERSTANDING THE SELF

AF655403

UNDERSTANDING THE SELF

Dr. Sunita Arya
Associate Professor, C. R. College of Education
Rohtak

Dr. Indu Bala Tehlan
Assistant Professor, C. R. College of Education
Rohtak

The Readers Paradise
New Delhi

UNDERSTANDING THE SELF

© 2017, 2020, 2023 Publisher

ISBN - 978-93-85958-59-5

All rights reserved. No part of this book may be reproduced in any form or by any means without written permission of the Publisher.
(All enquiries to be made to the Authors)

Published by
The Readers Paradise
103, 4787/23, Ansari Road,
Darya Ganj, New Delhi - 110002
011-23246222, 09811197091, 9654444181
thereadersparadisesales@gmail.com
www.thereadersparadise.com

Type Setting
Sanya Computers

Printed in India
Balaji Offset

Contents

PURPOSE OF THIS BOOK

The purpose of this book is to provide a resourse for integrated understanding of human self and personality in context of self development. It will help in understanding of inner self and know oneself as a person and as a teacher, through conscious ongoing reflection. Students, parents and teachers may have the mistaken impression that meditation and yoga is a religious practice. Self identity may be marginalized because of misconceptions and we forget to understand in the pace of development that

WHO AM I?

The emphasis of this book is on how identifying of self, knowing self esteem, our strengths and weaknesses conflict resolutions and managing stress helps an individual in developing in a sound way. The book provides instructions to safely teach soft skills to promote sensibilities that help to live in peace and harmony with one's surroundings. This book will enhance the students and teachers to appreciate the philosophy of yoga and provide an effective practical approach of various yogic practices and meditation. It is an attempt that will give a conscious direction to the lives of the readers.

Unit I
Knowing One's True Potential

Chapter - 1

Self Identity

Self identity is the way you look at yourself and your relationship to the world. Self identity makes us understand yourself. Self identity is composed of relatively permanent self-assessments, such as personality attributes, one's occupation and hobbies, awareness of one's physical attributes.

The self identity is not restricted to the present. It includes past selves and future selves. Future selves represent individuals' ideas of what they might become, what they would like to become, and what they are afraid of becoming. They correspond to hopes, fears, standards, goals, and threats. Possible selves may function as incentives for future behavior and they also provide an evaluative and interpretative context for the current view of self.

Each person is unique to them, and no one is perfect. In fact most people do not have a clear and conscious understanding of what they are.

Yourself identity is surrounded by your boundary which filters both outward and inward experience you have to the world.

As the life experiences come around you make decisions based on your boundaries, it increases your sense of self esteem and makes a stronger character of which you are in yourself identity. You are able to clearly define the limits of the extent of your control on self.

THE SELF

The central nucleus around which the personality develops is the self. The self is an organization within the individual which is unique and continuing. The self is a matter of experience or an object of knowledge. You may also describe yourself as to physique, intelligence, social skills, attitudes and belief systems or in simple way we can say the self is a point between past and future and it also includes unconscious components.

ANALYSIS OF SELF

The term 'self' has been used in many different ways which are given as:

1. Bodily Sense: The image of one's body, of one's muscular movements, as in sports, of one's agility or clumsiness, etc. These form a continuing core around which the embryonic self can develop, and this is an important component of self.
2. Self-identity: I remember my thoughts and actions of yesterday, and of years ago; consciously I am aware of and believe in my continuity. Subjectively I am certain that I am a continuing unity.
3. Ego Enhancement: Most, of the people show pride, selfishness, narcissism, and self-love. There is an almost universal tendency for the individual to strive to become more important, to be the center of attention, to be

observed and respected.

4. Ego Extension: Each self begins to attach to itself physical possessions (my home is part of my ego), social groups (my church, my labor union, my nation are part of me), a profession and other belongings. An attack on one of these is perceived as an attack on the self.
5. Self-image: The self as seen by itself, the person's phenomenal or conscious self. Even this may be subdivided into one's image of himself as he "really" is, and his ideal self-image, that which he would like to be.
6. Self-oriented Striving: It refers to the intensely motivated effort involved in self-expression and also includes the people who voluntarily accept pain and discomfort in pursuit of a dream.

ASPECTS OF INNER SELF

Turning inward is the self knowledge and it is being in touch with the world through our senses so that you have a clear picture of yourself in the world.

The Ways of Inner Self Development are given as.

1. The inputs of your senses.
2. Your thoughts—those you experience and those you generate.
3. Your feelings—what you feel now, and what you have felt at other times.
4. Your memories—what you recall of your life and work.
5. Your visions—products of your imagination, what you create.

6. Your assumptions—the concepts about yourself, others, and the world that you believe to be true.
7. Your values—the attitudes, behavior, and convictions that you consider important and use to guide your life.
8. Your intuition—what you sense to be true even without evidence to support you.
9. Belief—what you believe about the mysteries of life that are difficult to answer.

Turning inward is most easily conducted solitude that allows you to concentrate on your inner experience without interruption. Once you are relaxed and focus, you can turn your attention to any of these above themes and practice with them.

There is no upper limit to practice for any of them, even something as simple as listening. And as we enhance our experience of ourselves, the same process is developing who we are.

Remember to be aware of any discomfort you feel when you are working with your inner self. We cannot, and do not, take any responsibility for what you will actually experience because people are all so different. So monitor yourself. Stop if you feel any stress and, if necessary, seek professional help.

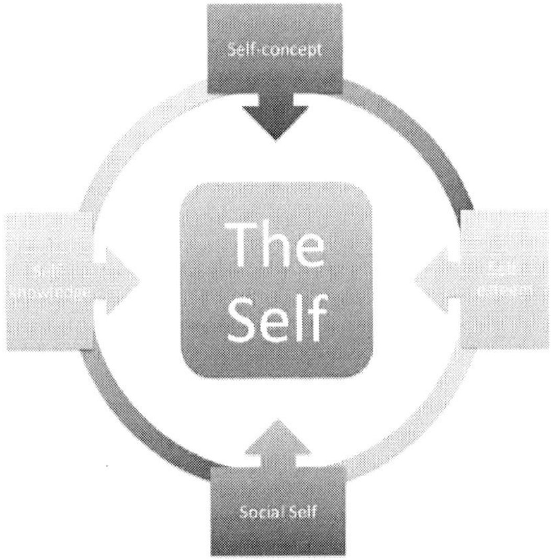

SELF DEVELOPMENT STRATEGIES

The self development strategies are divided into eight categories, which cover all the quadrants of living: spiritual, mental, emotional, and physical (actions). These areas are not completely discreet and separate, but overlaps each other which are given as:

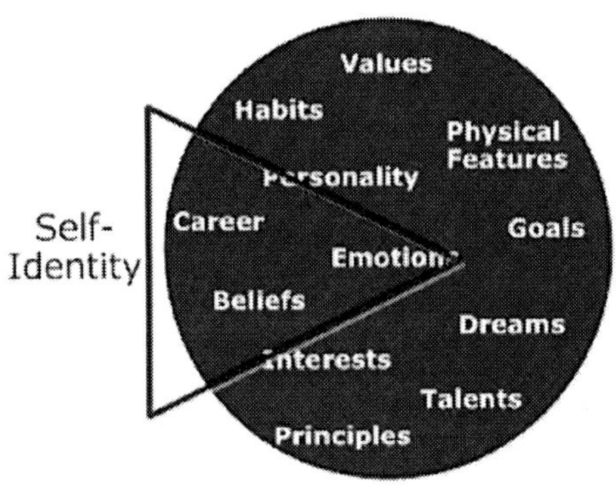

1. **Self Acceptance**– It means understanding who you are and accepting your faults. It's only after you begin to accept yourself that you can begin to change and grow into the person you want. Self acceptance also means accepting the level and pace of your growth, and giving yourself permission to be you, and permission to fail. Self Awareness forms a large part of self acceptance, as you develop.

2. **Self Respect**– Self respect means taking care of yourself and treating yourself right. This includes not just the actions you take but also how you talk to yourself. You're going to be talking to yourself, feeding yourself image and subconscious with messages of who you are.

3. **Self Esteem**– It is the value you place yourself. Recognizing and affirming that you are good enough, worthwhile and valuable.

4. **Self Belief**– It means trusting yourself and having faith in your judgment, skills, and yourself as a person.

5. **Self Love**– Self love means if you falling in love a large proportion of that are the same with confidence. Confidence and happiness are usually synonymous, just like love is a powerfully positive and blissful emotion. Loving yourself includes liking yourself.

6. **Self Assurance**– This is being aware of your purpose and being one to validate yourself, rather than looking to others to validate us is a major part of self assurance. A difference between self assurance and self belief is a kin. Self Assurance just knows that you'll succeed at what you do; self belief knows that regardless of the outcome, you'll be okay. Both are necessary and complimentary. Self belief is what keeps you going; self assurance is

what gets you there.

7. **Self Determination**– It is freedom and total control of your reality. With Self Determinism you are the ultimate authority in your life, deciding what your values and beliefs are, and then acting in accordance with them. You make the rules of your own reality.

8. **Self Admiration**– The word admiration over pride because of the negative consequences usually associated with the word. It's okay to be proud of who you are, to acknowledge and celebrate the great things you've done.

STEPS TO DETOXIFY YOUR INNER SELF

We have bloated with all the negative thoughts that we have created for you. We have been under deep pressure and felt so greasy of trouble and wanted some good shower of relaxation and we made a decision to crave to dip you in a river to cleanse all the troubles attached to us.

It is true that we need to detoxify our bodies with all the

junks around in what we eat and what we have in the environment. So we need to cleanse inner self with negativity.

There are five steps for cleansing our inner self

1. Compose yourself

Psychotherapists recommend a breathing exercise to compose oneself coming from any stressful situation. "Take five deep breaths, holding each one to a count of five before releasing it. Clear your thoughts completely and repeat to yourself "I am relaxed" whenever a stressful thought tries to make its way into your head."

Even one deep breath helps us to change our attitudes. It is just like gaining some courage when we breathe deeply and spewing out the fear when we breathe out.

2. Make a personal inventory

You can ask yourself these questions and make list in a notebook:

- What are the things that bother me often?
- What are the things that I do well and bring the best in me and in those that are important to me?

Applying this myself, I am always on the lookout for emotions or thoughts that occupy my mind a lot of times. They can be issues or disappointments that are borne out of my own expectation and not of anyone else.

3. Explore self-acceptance

There are many facets in our life where we know we perform our worse. Yet, this is not a pleasant thing to face, we deny it to ourselves. So these weak parts of ourselves are often neglected and are not nurtured.

According to Leon Seltzer People explore those parts of themselves that they have not yet accepted. He says "it's only when we stop judging ourselves that we can secure a more positive sense of who we are."

I unconsciously denied those inner rumblings that shaped some of my subconscious thoughts that included self-criticisms. I have been aware of those inner criticisms that I have learned to accept myself for who I am.

4. Throw out unnecessary things

As we make our personal inventory and explore self-acceptance, there is a lot of clutter that we carry deep inside of us. These are things that are useless, old and unnecessary. You can start crossing them out of the list if they are trifles. What could they be?

- Reminiscing old relationships that turned sour.
- Regrets and resentments-the what-is, what-should ask and what-could ask.
- Personal tastes or inclination that are unnecessary.

When I find myself in these situations, I throw them out of the bin once and for all and forget them telling myself gently, "Cut it off, you have better things to do."

5. Self-denial

The last step to inner self detoxify would be setting out oneself back into the real world and practice a pinch of mortification that is, self-control in small and even trivial matters.

6. Moving on

Going through this, I have developed a healthier inner self and enabled me to move higher in the path to self-improvement.

At the end we can say "To be aware of oneself is to have a concept of oneself" that is called as self concept.

****

Chapter - 2

Self Concept

SELF CONCEPT

Self-concept is the image of us and how someone thinks about, evaluates or perceives themselves. Self-image is influenced by our interactions with important people in our lives.

Definitions

"Self-concept is our perception or image of our abilities and our uniqueness. At first one's self-concept is very general and changeable and as we grow these self-perceptions become much more organized, detailed, and specific."

"A self-concept is a collection of beliefs about one's own nature, unique qualities, and typical behavior so we say self-concept is our mental picture of our self. It is a collection of self-perceptions. For example, a self-concept includes such beliefs as. 'I am pretty' or 'I am hard working. 'Such belief are called self-concept."

According to Baumeister (1990) "The individual's belief about himself or herself, including the person's attributes and who and what the self is".

According to Lewis (1990) self concept has two aspects:

1. The Existential Self

This is basic part of the self-scheme or self-concept; it separate and distinct from others and the awareness of the constancy of the self. (Bee, 1992)

The child realizes that they exist as a separate entity from others and they continue to exist over time and space. The awareness of the existential self begins as young as two to three months old and arises in part due to the relation the child has with the world e.g. the child smiles and some ones smiles back, or the child touches a mobile and sees it moving.

2. The Categorical Self

The child realizes that they exist as a separate experiencing being, after that child become aware that he or she is also an object in the world just as other objects including people have properties that can be experienced (big, small, red, smooth and so on). The self can also be put into categories such as age, gender size or skill.

SELF CONCEPT IS OF THREE TYPES

1. **The individual self:** It consists of attributes and personality traits that differentiate us from other individuals for example e.g. 'introvert person.
2. **The relational self:** It is defined by our relationships with others e.g. sister, brother, uncle etc.
3. **The collective self:** It reflects our membership in social group's e.g. British, Indian and Chinese etc.

Components of Self-Concept

Self-concept is composed of two parts: personal identity and social identity.

1. Personal identity– It includes personality traits and other characteristics that make each person unique.
2. Social identity– It includes the groups we belong to including our community, religion, college, and other groups.

There are six specific domains related to self-concept

- Social– It is the ability to interact with others
- Competence– It is the ability to meet basic needs
- Affect– It is the awareness of emotional states
- Physical– It is the feelings about looks, health, physical condition, and overall appearance
- Academic– It is the success or failure in school
- Family– In it how well we functions within the family unit.

Part of Self-concept

It consists of three parts

1. Self image
2. Self esteem
3. Ideal self

1. Self-image

Self-image, it means how we see ourselves. It is not necessary that self-image match with reality. People have an inflated self-image and they believe that they are better than really they are. Conversely, people are also having negative self-images and perceive or weaknesses. For example, a teenage boy believes that he is socially awkward but he is really quite charming. A teenage girl believes that she is overweight, but she is really quite thin.

Each individual's self-image includes his physical characteristics, personality traits and social roles.

Self-image may also be defined as it is our mental picture that we have which describes the characteristics of the self including intelligent, beautiful, ugly, talented, selfish, and kind. These characteristics form a collective representation of our assets and as we see them.

Self-image is not permanent but it is dynamic and changeable and it is a process which occurs over a lifetime. A healthy self-image starts with learning to accept and love ourselves and being accepted and loved by others.

Development of Self Image

Self-image is a product of learning. Nature and Nurture influences our self-image. They are mirrors reflecting back to us an image of ourselves. Our experiences with others such as teachers, friends, and family add to the image in the mirror. Relationships reinforce our thinking and feeling about ourselves. The image we see in the mirror may be a real or distorted of who we really are. On the basis of image we see in the mirror, we develop either a positive or a negative self-image. The strengths and weaknesses we have affect how we act today. We continuously evaluate ourselves in multiple domains such as physical appearance, performance, and relationships. With a positive self-image we recognize our potentials. With a negative self-image; we focus on our weaknesses, failure and imperfections. A positive self-image can enhance our physical, mental, social, emotional, and spiritual well-being. Conversely a negative self-image can decrease our satisfaction and ability to function in these areas. Self image is important because how we think about ourselves affect how we feel about ourselves and how we interact with others.

Steps to Foster A Positive Self-Image

Make a list of your positive qualities

- Ask others to describe your positive qualities
- Define personal goals and objectives that are reasonable and measurable
- Refrain from comparing yourself to others
- Develop your strengths
- Learn to love yourself
- Give positive affirmations
- Remember that you are unique

Change negative thoughts to positive one by focusing on the positive thoughts and forgetting negative things that happen to you.

2. Self-esteem

Self-esteem or self worth– Means how much we value our self. A number of factors can impact self-esteem, including how we compare ourselves to others and how others respond to us. When people respond positively to our behavior, we develop positive self-esteem. When we compare ourselves to others and find ourselves lacking, it can have a negative impact on our self-esteem. So Self esteem refers to the extent to which we like accept or approve of ourselves or how much we value ourselves. It always involves a degree of evaluation and we may have either a positive or a negative view of ourselves.

High Self Esteem

This tends to lead to

- Confidence in our own abilities
- Self acceptance
- Not worrying about what others think
- Optimism

Low Self Esteem

This tends to lead to

- Lack of confidence
- Want to be/look like someone else
- Always worrying what others might think
- Pessimism effect.

According to Argyle there are 4 major factors that influence self esteem.

(1) **The Reaction of Others**– If people admire us, flatter us, listen attentively and agree with us we tend to develop a positive self-image. If they avoid us, neglect us; tell us things about ourselves that we don't want to hear we develop a negative self-image.

(2) **Comparison with Others**– If the people compare ourselves with others who are more successful, happier, richer, better looking than ourselves then we develop a negative self image but if they are less

successful then us our image will be positive.

(3) **Social Roles**– Some social roles carry prestige e.g. doctor, airline pilot, TV. Presenter, footballer etc. this promotes self-esteem. Some other roles carry stigma like mental hospital patient or unemployed person.

(4) **Identification**– Roles aren't just "out there." They also become part of our personality i.e. we identity with the positions we occupy, the roles we play and the groups we belong to.

3. Ideal Self

Ideal self, means how we wish we could be. In many cases we see ourselves and how we would like to see ourselves does not quite match up.

If there is a mismatch between how you see yourself and what you'd like to be, this affects how much you value yourself. So there is an intimate relationship between self-image, ego-ideal and self-esteem.

According to Michael Argyle there are mainly four factors which influence Ideal self:

- The ways in which other react to us
- How we think we compare with others
- Our social roles
- The extent to which we identify with other people

Ideal Self is of Two Types

1. Incongruence
2. Congruence

1. **Incongruence:** A person's ideal self may not be consistent with what actually happens in life and experiences of the person. Hence, there is a difference between a person's ideal self and actual experience. This is called incongruence e.g. some students believe that they are great at academics, but their school records tell a different story.

2. **Congruence:** If a person's ideal self and actual experiences are similar, then a state of congruence Occurs. The development of congruence is dependent on unconditional positive regard. According to Roger's when a person achieves self-actualization they must be in a state of congruence. E.g. unconditional love helps to foster congruence. Children who experience such love feel no need to continually distort their memories in order to believe that other people will love and accept them as they are.

Characteristics of a congruent person include:

- Openness to experience
- A flexible self-concept
- Unconditional regard for the self
- The ability to live in harmony with others

Personal Construct

A personal construct is your personal way of looking at life, towards the world, and people around you, based upon your experiences. You "construct" or build your outlook based upon your personal experiences in life and your reactions to them.

Your personal constructs or beliefs about life, the world and others shapes the way you make decisions about how to act, speak, think and live your life. If you get a burnt from touching a grill you build a “construct” your rule that says– Don’t touch hot grills.

So it is the way I think, determines how I respond to the world around me – people, places and things. Then the response of feedback you get in life conditions you to make more “constructs” or ways of understanding and looking at the world around you.

It is the rules of life that you personally make up for yourself, as you go along your way in life based on your experiences in life.

Personal Construction and Friendship

A personal construct that defines a friend as someone you trust and with whom you can enjoy the following:

- Sharing personal information about yourself
- Feeling a sense of loyalty
- Spending time and enjoying interests and activities
- Feeling a sense of supportiveness and encouragement

Our personal constructs toward friendship are affected by the culture in which we live and reflect the cultural values that are identified with being a friend. Popular forms of entertainment have reflected culturally and shared values about friendship. Generally it is found that people are likely to form friendships with those who are perceived as being honest, responsible, and fun loving, and intelligent. These above four values ascribed to close friends. Some other values also found in close friends are being creative, cultured and dynamic.

Nonetheless, you may develop a very unique personal construct that applies to a particular friendship. One friendship may be characterized by powerful bonds of emotional interdependency, while another may be distinguished by a special brand of humor that is uniquely shared.

Personal constructs are developed throughout one's social life based on the way one perceives events, perceptions that will direct one's behavior in future, A personal construct is a way of comparing how things are similar and different.

People are varied. Some people will prefer to lean to the vertical side of personal development, while others lean to the lateral side.

****

Chapter - 3

Adult Child Gap

MEANING OF ADULT - CHILD GAP

Adult child gap is nothing but certain psychological and emotional gap between parents or elder people and the younger ones. Bulging adult child gap creates misunderstanding and lack of attachment between the parents and children. The success of parenting lies in how effectively they avoid the generation gap between parents and children.

Adult child gap may also be defined as the new involving trends which cannot be followed by their parents in spite of being good or bad as well. This situation can be handled by acquiring proper communication skills between parents and their children that the new things involving in our society would be captured by them. Even if children have problems will carry on some blind traditions can be resolved by using proper communication skills. The important thing in the communication between their parents and children is the level of thinking as well as level of understanding.

It is the result of the fast paced development of the society and also due to technology, dating habits, social media, dressing taboos, superstitions. In earlier times two or more generations live in the same lifestyle and in the same environments and under the same roof. But today, nearest past is very much outdated and the world is more advanced each day. Parents do not know about modern technologies and equipments which their children use. So the parents need to cope with their children to overcome the generation gap.

SUGGESTIONS OR ADVICE FOR THE PARENTS TO COPE WITH ADULT CHILD GAP

1. Being update is the only way to cope up with the adult child gap. If we are asked doubt by our children and if our answer is that we do not know, then we may be counted outdated parents. To avoid this situation, try to be update with the latest information and technologies. Never make your child feel that we are an old fashion parents. When children express their feelings, understand them in the modern world context.

2. Many parents are mistaken of evaluating their children by comparing their age with that of parent's when he/she was in the same age. When a parent was in sixteenth, he/ she might need a bicycle, but their child of same age may ask for a scooter. Understanding the requirements of present time and lifestyles of modern children will help you in evaluating your children and taking right decisions without making their child feel that you are outdated parents.

3. Make friendship with their children instead of beings rude parents'. Let them to express all their_feelings with you. So you can cope up with the generation gap by learning the feelings and requirement of the children.

4. In fact, there is no global standard of attitudes. Different people may have different attitudes. But, when such

difference in attitudes come under the same roof, then it affects communications and active relationships. Knowing it better is the right way of avoiding it.

5. Bridging the adult child gap between parent and children is essential. Parents often contribute their share in digging gap between parents and children by pushing the kid's beyond their limits. This happens when parents either demands higher than the limits of the child or pushes the child beyond the economical or social limits of parents. This makes the child going astray from the lifestyle and status of parents. If child grows higher, parents should grow in attitudes and thinking levels to cope up with the child.

6. Never make your child feelings ashamed of the parents. If he expresses his desires on the look or behavior of his parents, be ready to change yourself. For example, if your child says that his friend's parents comes in a luxury car, then your buying another luxury car is stupidity but when your child says that you speak more loudly or dress up in old fashion then you can think about changing yourself. In this way you can cope up with the expectations of the children and always be updated.

7. As your children growing up, their thinking level change; the way they look at the world change; the way they express feelings change. So parents should learn to understand the growth of the children.

8. Love and respect for each other plays an important role in bridging an adult child gap. If one finds the other showing his affection towards him, then the other would start to respect him.

9. Convincing your parents without abashing yourselves or them through conversation, it could do you some good.
10. Each side should hold a compromising attitude towards the other or they try to live by compromising, they should make them understand each other well.
11. Asking your uncles or aunts who are of intermediate generation to help you, it can work wonders.
12. Be veracious with your parents and don't pretend to hide information.
13. Explain the pros and cons of your decisions and display clarity in what you want to do.

At the end it also becomes the responsibility of the younger generations to cope the generation gap by changing himself in a controlled and smooth manner. After all it is the younger generation that has the first hand experience of today's time in their youth.

****

Chapter - 4

Personality and its Determinants

'PERSONALITY'

Meaning of Personality: The term 'Personality' is derived from the Latin word 'Persona', which means a theatrical mask used by actors or worn by actors to indicate their role in theatrical play.

People ordinarily think that personality means reputation or physical attractiveness of a person. It does not simply mean the outward appearance of a person. In addition to the outer self, it also refers to her or his inner self. So, personality is the totality of a man, both his inner and outer qualities interacting with each other.

According to Cloninger and Phares– "Personality is a pattern of characteristic feelings, thoughts and behaviors that persists across time and situations".

According to Nelson and Miller– "Personality is an individual's unique and relatively stable patterns of behavior, thoughts and emotions".

According to Friedman and Schustack– "Personality are the psychological forces that make people uniquely themselves".

According to Warren– "Personality is the entire mental

organization of a human being at any stage of development." This refers to the organization of personal traits.

Personality also refers to qualities within a person, characteristics of a person's behavior or both.

According to Allport– "Personality is the dynamic organization within the individual of those psycho-physical systems that determine characteristics, behavior and thought."

Meaning of the key words used in above definition is given below:

1. **Dynamic:** "Dynamic" refers to the constantly changing nature of personality.
2. **Organization:** "Organization" emphasizes the patterning of the independent parts of the personality structure, each of which has a special relation to the whole. A normal healthy personality is a highly correlated structured person. The abnormal personality shows disorganization
3. **Psycho-physical systems:** A "psycho-physical system" is composed of habits, attitudes, emotional states, sentiments, motives and beliefs, all of which are psychological but have a physical basis in the individual's neural, glandular, or general bodily states.
4. **Determine:** The word "determine" emphasizes the motivational role of the psycho-physical systems.
5. **Unique:** Unique means adjustment of every person is unique in time, place, and quality.

CHARACTERISTICS OF PERSONALITY

Personality has so many characteristics. Some of these characteristics are mentioned below:

1. It is stable.
2. It is dynamic.
3. It is unique and specific.
4. It is all pervasive.
5. It is assessable and measurable.
6. It exhibits self-consciousness.
7. It includes all behavior patterns-cognitive, affective and conative.

PERSONALITY DETERMINANTS

"Personality determinants" are the forces which modify and channelize the expression of our basic needs and which, in fact, predetermine certain needs and motives. An individual is the by-product of constant interaction of hereditary and environmental factors. These two factors contribute to the development of an individual. The individual is like or different from other individuals in performance and personality is due to these two factors hereditary and environment and a few other important forces that determine the structuring, developing, shaping, and organizing of personality are called personality determined which are further divided into two categories :

1. Biological Determinants
2. Socio-cultural Determinants

Biological Determinants

Biological-constitutional determinants are those which are inherited like traits, tendencies and limitations they have to do with the physiological characteristics that affect our lives. The organism is born with certain biological inheritance. The biological inheritance includes both factors genetic and physiological factor. Genetic factors are basic that determine the personality development of an individual. Physiological factors are the determinants such as ductless glands; nervous system, emotions, and motivation all play an important role in the development of an individual's personality and which are explained below:

1. **Glandular Development and Activity of Ductless Glands or Endocrine Glands**: Glandular development and activity affect personality in a number of ways. Ductless or endocrine glands are so called because they discharge their secretions or hormones directly into the bloodstream or send their secretions directly to the blood without ducts (tubes), influence the behavior of individuals according to their balance or imbalance. Each gland secretes one or more types of hormones. Hormones secreted through these glands (such as thyroid, adrenal, sex glands, pituitary, pancreas, etc.) have an impact on personality. Over secretion (hyper-secretion) or under secretion (hypo-secretion) by any of these glands may exert a tremendous influence upon an individual's development and consequently upon his personality (Hoskins, 1933) insufficient secretions from the thyroid gland, for example, can make a person lethargic and sluggish.

2. **Heredity**: Heredity is an important determinant of personality. "Heredity" means the biological transmission of genetic characteristics from parent to offspring or child. Some characteristic of personality such as intelligence, interests, talents, emotional expressions, stress tolerance etc. It does not completely determine any characteristic or trait but it provides basis of potential for the development of any personality trait. Heredity influences physique, motor-sensory equipment and level of intelligence. Recently, it has been established that certain diseases and temperamental characteristics are also inherited from forefathers or ancestors.

3. **Nervous System:** The nervous system is one of the important determinants of personality. The autonomic nervous system plays an important role. Several Psychologists have documented the role of nervous system in extraversion, introversion, neuroticism – the important traits of personality and in emotions.

4. **Physique or Physical Structure:** Another important biological determinant affecting personality is physique. "Physique" is the structure and anatomical organization of the body. Physique constitutes size of the body, complexion of the skin, general health, physical deformities, etc. A balanced combination of all these features is an eye-catching and attractive personality. But owing to poor physique, people are subject to humiliation, bias, and prejudice, which arouses inferiority complex in them. It is also observed that people's behavior towards other individuals is modified, to some extent, according to their physique or physical structure.

5. **Temperament:** Individual's first personality is temperamental in nature and it is on this initial behavior

pattern that the framework of his personality is erected. The personality of an infant is constituted almost entirely by its temperament. The temperament of an infant is not only an important ingredient in her or his budding or growing personality, but it directly affects the emotional climate of her or his family, which in turn, has effect on her or his personality. The emotional climate not only tends to persist into childhood but also forms the basis of the child's expectations of herself or himself. In this way, the temperament of the infant sets up waves of feelings, this constitutes the forces mounding her or his personality during its earliest stage.

6. **Body Type:** Personality traits are caused by the type of body structure. It may be that to have a certain kind of temperament and to grow up in a certain kind of emotional climate means that one will develop a certain kind of body. Drugs, deficiency of different vitamins in the body, long illnesses also because some changes in the personality.

Socio-cultural Determinants

Some of the important socio-cultural determinants affecting personality of an individual are discussed below:

1. **Home**: The home environment plays an important role in shaping the personality pattern of an individual. In fact, home is a place where the foundations of personality are laid. Family is the major socializing agent during early years of life in the development of personality. Children coming from homes where good morale pattern dominated were better adjusted, more independent, and more satisfactorily related to their parents than were the average adolescents of the group. The child learns various

socially valued skills, etiquettes, manners, habits, beliefs, attitudes, ways of adjusting to problems, and values in the family. Child rearing practices adopted by parents, rewards and punishments used, parental expectations, parental attitudes, interpersonal relationships help in determining and developing personality traits. Many other factors, such as size of the family, ordinal position of the child, sex-distribution, sibling rivalry, sex compositional pattern of siblings in the family, etc. are also important familial correlates of personality. Disturbed family structure exposes the children to stressors, conflicts and feelings of insecurity and rejection. Those coming from homes showing family discord pattern were generally, poorly adjusted in their social environment. So, a congenial home atmosphere with good relations with parents and other family members is essential for a healthy personality.

2. **Neighborhood**: People, who live in the neighborhood, influence the development of personality. Neighborhood is like second home where the child interacts with other children. This interaction helps the child to learn various traits, skills, and responses. A stable neighborhood permits the development of cooperation, sympathy, affection, and caring attitude.

3. **School**: School, a primary social group, is another factor that influences personality because a significant part of a child's life is spent in school where the child interacts with teachers, classmates, schoolmates, and school administrators. The institutional rule and regulations, social climate, playground activities, competitiveness and instructional process are important factors for the makeup of child's personality. The school has an important role

to shape, mould, and regulate the personality of children by creating better emotional atmosphere, better teaching methods, and by providing guidance and counseling.

4. **Economic Factors**: Economic factors greatly determine some of the important personality traits. Poverty of parents and lack of money to fulfill the legitimate needs of their children lead directly to frustration. Socio-economic inferiority is a well-known cause of the development of undesirable personality traits among young people. These adverse effects of poverty on cognitive functioning seem to occur as a function of a variety of factors associated with poverty, including poor physical health or low birth weight at birth, higher risk of prenatal exposure to drugs, higher risk of lead poisoning and less cognitive stimulation in the home environment.

5. **Ordinal Position in the Family**: Ordinal positions in the family-whether oldest, middle, youngest or only child-influences the personality pattern to a great extent. The birth order of the child fixes her or his status in the family which decides her or his roles that affect the personality. Oldest sons in patriarchal families frequently develop "crown-prince" characteristics of behavior; they look upon themselves as "assistant fathers", are dominant, have a strong sense of responsibility, are self-sufficient, and tend to take themselves very seriously. The birth of another child in the family has an important influence on the first child, since it takes away her or his monopoly in affection and sometimes she or he is neglected altogether. Hence, she or he feels jealous with the younger child and tries to regain her or his rights. Frequently, the oldest child is the object of more anxiety on the part of

the parents than are younger children; she or he is also likely to be more jealous. So, an eldest child may be of authoritarian type of personality. The youngest child in the family is treated with love and affection by everyone, hence she or he becomes over dependent. A single child may be of careless temperament.

6. **Early Childhood Experiences**: Childhood experiences are decisive determinants of personality. In fact, every experience from the moment of conception till death affects the personality. Traumatic experiences or psychic traumas in the childhood influence our perceptions of ourselves and our environment. Feeding, weaning, toilet training, child-rearing practices, parents' attitudes, inconsistent discipline play an important role in the development of personality.

7. **Inter-Personal Relations** : An individual interacts with different members of the society as she or he grows and these interpersonal interaction and relations are important means which help in the development of certain social personality characteristics and traits, which in turn result in dynamic changes in response tendencies to make better adjustment. When social roles are conflicting, unclear, or uncomfortable, or when an individual is unable to achieve a satisfactory role in a group, healthy personality development may be impaired.

8. **Parenting Styles**: Parenting styles have a significant impact on a child's development. These styles vary in the degree of parental warmth (amount of support, encouragement, and affection versus shame, rejection, and hostility) and in the degree of parental control (extent of discipline and monitoring versus being largely unsupervised).

Parenting style is of four types which are given as:

1. **Authoritative parenting style:** In authoritative parenting style, parents are both very warm and set clear limits and restrictions to the behavior of children and this parenting style is related with positive outcomes.
2. **Authoritarian parenting style:** In authoritarian parenting style, parents are high on control and low on warmth. This parenting style is related with negative outcomes; conflicted, irritable, moody children, poor, social and cognitive skills, and aggressive behavior.
3. **Permissive-Indulgent parenting style:** In permissive-indulgent parenting style, parents are high on warmth, low on control and discipline. This style of parenting is associated with impulsive and aggressive behavior and children. Much permissiveness and little discipline in the home is associated with antisocial and aggressive behavior. Overly indulged children are spoiled, selfish, impatient, inconsiderate, and demanding. Indulged children enter readily into inter-personal relationships, but they exploit people for their own purposes in the same way that they have learned to exploit their parents.
4. **Neglectful-uninvolved parenting style:** In neglectful-uninvolved parenting style, parents are low both on warmth and control. In neglectful parenting style, infants or children suffer from inadequate care at home. Parents typically neglect or devote little attention to their child or children and are generally rejecting. Parental rejection of a child may be

demonstrated by parents in various ways – by physical neglect, denial of love or affection, lack of interest in child's activities and achievements, failure to spend time with the child, lack of respect for the child's feelings and rights, cruel and abusive treatment. This deprivation and rejection may lead to retarded growth and development, physiological disturbance, poor linguistic development, personality disorders, anger, and aggression.

9. **Child Abuse:** Abuse (physical or sexual or both) of children has also been associated with negative effect on the development of child's victim's personality. Abused children often have a tendency to be overly aggressive, socially withdrawn, self-injurious and suicidal behaviors, problems in social and emotional functioning, impaired relationships, depression, insecure attachment, relationship difficulties, anxiety, lower IQ and reading ability, lower academic achievement, inability to trust, and low self-esteem.

10. **Value Patterns:** The broader aspects of personality are shaped by the value patterns of the culture. The culture determines what the standards of right and wrong behavior shall be – that is, what the norms are – what is important in the environment, what kind of behavior shall be rewarded or punished, and what the rewards and penalties shall be. The personalities of individuals in our culture are also molded by the pattern of values is the core of our middle class ideology.

11. **Self-Concept:** Self-concept influences our personality development in two ways. One is that if other people hold high positive attitudes towards us, this enhances

our self-image and self-acceptance. The other is that if others hold negative attitudes toward us, it creates feelings of worthlessness or triviality and consequently may lead to self-defense or withdrawal from social situations.

12. **Sexual Function or Sex Roles:** The role of sex is well-defined in each culture – the behavior, attitudes, and personal qualities society expects of each person according to her or his sex. E.g. Women are born to be passive, dependent, and submissive, whereas men are born to be active, dominant, and aggressive. The personality characteristics that we associate with womanhood (submission, co-operation, aesthetic expression etc.) are not so much biologically determined as they are the result of what the culture has led us to expect of women and what women have come to expect of themselves. Similarly, many of the personality characteristics we have come to associate with manhood (dominance, independence, aggression, etc.) are the result of the fact that our culture expects men to play competitive occupational roles in our patriarchal society. Nevertheless, the fact that women are smaller, weaker, slighter, and are peculiarly equipped for child-bearing has a pronounced effect on their personalities, irrespective of the culture they belong to.

13. **Minority or Racial Group:** Being one of the unprivileged or dependent minority or backward or racial group has a considerable impact on the personality of that individual. Members of such groups at one time reflected and still reflect in their personality, the bias, prejudice, discrimination, and

injustice constantly directed against them by the members of the majority or privileged group. Some of the members belonging to these minority groups accept their inferior status in the society and do not protest against it, while others resist, protest, revolt, and develop aggressive attitude, which result in the social changes taking place rapidly and also in transformations of the society.

14. **Culture:** "Culture" refers to the total activities of a society. It leaves permanent impressions on the personality of an individual. All the behavior patterns which the parents transmit to their children are cultural products. Culture is in fact, the ground from which personality emerges.

The importance of cultural forces in the development of personality is very great. Personality is determined by culture which represents the environment in its totality. Customs, traditions, rituals, standards, norms, values, needs, attitudes, beliefs, religious faiths, aspirations, childhood training, and ways of living of an individual are regulated by the culture she or he belongs to. Culture regulates our lives at every turn.

THE PSYCHODYNAMIC APPROACHES TO PERSONALITY

Sigmund Freud, an Austrian Physician, developed psychodynamic and Psychoanalytic approaches to personality. The Psychodynamic approach is one of them which are based on the idea that personality is motivated by inner forces and conflicts about which people have little awareness and over which they have no control. Personality is composed of three element Id, ego and superego which are given as:

The Id, Ego and Superego

According to Sigmund Freud's personality is composed of three elements. These three elements of personality are id, the ego and the superego. These elements are not physical divisions of the brain but work together to create complex human behaviors. These element interact effectively and determines the quality of an individual's mental health. When these element interact harmoniously-individual is well adjusted. When there is discontinuity-the individual is likely to be maladjusted.

The Id

- The id is the only component of personality that is present from birth.
- The human is born with an id, which is immature and illogical.
- This aspect of personality is entirely unconscious and includes of the instinctive and primitive behaviors.
- According to Freud, the id is the source of all psychic energy, making it the primary component of personality.
- It is unrealistic selfish and demanding working on Pleasure Principle.

Pleasure principle means id desires immediate gratification of all desires, wants, and needs. If these needs are not satisfied immediately it causes anxiety or tension. For example, an increase in hunger or thrust should produce an immediate attempt to eat or drink. The id is very important in infancy stage, because it ensures that an infant's needs are met. If infant is hungry or uncomfortable, he or she will cry until the demands of the id are met.

It is the immoral basic stuff of a man's personality that is hidden in the deep layers of her or his unconsciousness. Id has no value, no laws, and no rules, does not recognize right or wrong and considers only the satisfaction of its needs and appetites to be highly important.

According to Freud, the id tries to resolve the tension created by the pleasure principle through the primary process, which involves forming a mental image of the desired object as a way of satisfying the need.

The Ego

"Ego" is the rational part of the personality that mediates between the demands of the id and the constraints of the super-ego and the realities of the external world.

- According to Freud, the ego begins to develop soon after birth, but does not become apparent until the age of about six months.
- Ego does not develop until the id starts interacting with its environment but develops because of the need to deal with the outside world.
- The ego functions in the conscious, preconscious, and unconscious mind.

The ego operates according to the reality principle.

Reality principle means the recognition of the reality of the environment by the child, the growing awareness of its demands and the need to accommodate to them or trying to balance the demands of the unconscious mind with what is practical.

The ego also discharges tension created by unmet impulses through the secondary process called thinking. This include reasoning, planning, making evaluations and so on. In which the ego tries to find an object in the real world that matches the mental image created by the id's primary process. The strength and effectiveness of the ego is an important determinant of individual's adjustment.

The Superego

The third component of personality is the 'super ego' which includes individual's conscience, ideals, moral, and values, rules, principles and duties. So superego is the ethical or moral dimensions or attitudes of the personality.

- The superego is the aspect of personality that holds all of our internalized moral standards and ideals that we acquire from both parents and society–our sense of right and wrong.
- The superego provides guidelines for making judgments.
- According to Freud, the superego develops out of the ego's response to parental controls.
- The superego absorbs all the prohibitions, inhibitions and standards that are expressed by parents and society.

There are two parts of the superego

1. **The ego ideal**– It includes the rules and standards for good behaviors. These behaviors are those which are approved by parents and society. Obeying these rules leads to feelings of pride, value and accomplishment.
2. **The conscience**– It includes information about things

that are viewed as bad by parents and society. These behaviors are often forbidden and lead to bad consequences, punishments or feelings of guilt and remorse.

The superego acts to perfect and civilize our behavior. It works to suppress all unacceptable urges of the id and struggles to make the ego act upon idealistic standards rather that upon realistic principles. The superego is present in the conscious, preconscious and unconscious.

DEFENSE MECHANISM

According to Sigmund Freud defense mechanisms are the strategies by which ego unconsciously defends itself against undesirable thoughts; feeling or impulses. The defense mechanisms are further categorized which are given as

1. **Repression**– Repression means the mental process that functions to protect the individual from ideas, impulses and memories which would produce anxiety or guilt. It means preventing painful or dangerous thoughts from entering consciousness. Repression is also known as motivated forgetting. So it is an unconscious process where unacceptable impulses or feelings are purposefully forgotten in order to avoid the possible consequences of acting upon them, as well as to avoid the pain of being aware of them.

2. **Regression**– Regression means reverting to an earlier developmental state involving less mature behavior and responsible ability. When we are troubled, our behavior becomes more childish or primitive. For example– (1) sometimes 12 years old boy may show regression by thumb sucking or wet bed even though he never sucked

his thumb as an infant. When they need to spend some time in the hospital. (2) Sometimes a young lady might retreat to the security of her parent's home after her first quarrel with husband.

3. **Reaction formation**– It is the process by which unacceptable feelings or impulses are controlled by establishing the behavior patterns which are directly opposed to them. We can say it is a defense mechanism that replaces an unacceptable impulse by rigid adherence to a set of attitudes or beliefs that are the opposite of the unacceptable impulse. For example– a mother who bears an unwanted child may react to her feelings of guilt for not wanting the child by becoming extremely solicitous and over protective to convince both the child and herself.

4. **Rationalization**– Rationalization is a process to conceal the true motivations for one's actions, thoughts or feelings. It is a cognitive distortion of "the facts" to make an event or an impulse less threatening.

5. **Sublimation**– Sublimation is the process whereby primitive impulses are redirected and refined into new, learned, non-instinctive behavior. Or we can say it is the transforming of an unacceptable impulse, whether it is sex, anger, fear or whatever, into a socially acceptable, even productive form. E.g. Sometime a person suffering from a great deal of anxiety in a confusing world may become an organizer, a businessman or a scientist.

6. **Displacement**– "Displacement" is the transference of affect and desires from their original object or person to another object or person or it is the redirection of an impulse onto a substitute target e.g. (1) a man harassed and exploited by his boss at work place initiates an

argument with his wife or children at home. (2)Sometime a person who is frustrated by her or his superior or he may go home and kick the dog, beat up a family member, or engage in cross- burnings.

7. **Projection**– "Projection" means one's unacceptable behavior or characteristics to other. It is the process of getting rid of impulses that are objectionable to the ego by attributing the impulses to other people. It is also called displacement outward and is almost the complete opposite of turning against the self. It involves the tendency to see your own unacceptable desires in other people and it functions to protect oneself from anxiety e.g. a husband, a good and faithful one, finds himself terribly attracted to the flirtatious and beautiful lady next door. But rather acknowledge his own, hardly abnormal lust; he becomes increasingly jealous of his wife, constantly, worried about her faithfulness and so on.

8. **Denial**– "Denial" means protecting the self from an unpleasant reality by refusing to face it. It is a defense mechanism that denies thoughts, feeling, wishes or needs that causes anxiety and it involves blocking external events from awareness. If some situation is too much hard to handle, the person just refuses to experience it. This defense mechanism is commonly used by children.

****

Chapter - 5

Communication and Soft Skills

CONCEPT OF SOFT SKILLS

Know thyself is a term coined by the Great Greek philosopher Socrates meaning "Know Yourself ". Knowing yourself is a lifelong process. You need to remove all of the multiple personalities that you put on for different people and at different times. You need to get down to the core of your essence and then you get to rid of your own false self images and delusions.

You must live your lives in search of identifying your true self. You may not be able to know the full well of yourself still it is possible to know it is greater extent by knowing yourself, your strengths, weaknesses, fears and so on. To know yourself is to know yours own true identity.

Meaning of Soft Skills

Soft skills are essentially people skills-the non-technical, intangible, personality-specific skills that determine one's strengths. Soft skills revolve around personal relationships, character and attitude. By developing these skills, you can increase your work performance, build stronger relationships and work culture. Soft skills is a term often associated with a person's EQ (Emotional Intelligence Quotient) the cluster of personality traits, social graces, communication, language, personal habits, interpersonal skills etc. that characterize relationship with other people.

Soft Skills are the self development skills of an individual. Hard Skills on the other hand are more along the lines of what might appear on your resume – your education, experience and level of expertise.

IMPORTANCE OF SOFT SKILLS

Soft Skills play an important role for the success of an individual. Soft Skills complement the hard skills present in the individual. It is essential to be technically sound, but one should also have the ability to convey the idea to the masses in the simplest possible manner.

Soft Skills are Very Important

- To handle interpersonal relations
- To take appropriate decisions
- To communicate effectively
- To have good impression and impact to gain professional development

The impact of soft skills is very important on the life a student as well as for a professionals. Today graduates are academically competent and excellent with relation to hard skills but seriously lack in skills like 'team work', 'leadership'; quantitative aptitude and verbal reasoning. Students are facing adjustment problems with in self and with outside world due to lack of soft skills. Amongst the soft skills the most important are the communication skills.

SIGNIFICANCE OF SOFT SKILLS

Every individual has his own perception of Soft Skills. Whenever we talk about Soft Skills, the first thing that springs immediately to mind is – Communication Skills because that is the skill that is mostly lacking amongst individual of all ages and all categories. Almost all educational institutions force the students to pay more attention to technical subjects and leave the training of Soft Skills as secondary issue.

If Soft Skills are to be inculcated in an individual, we need to look onto the important factors shaping his character as well as his skills of communication.

ACQUISITION OF SOFT SKILLS

The first way to get enrolled on a Soft Skills training course on rhetoric, languages, presentation skills, conflict or cultural management. This is a well-proven concept with the advantage of having some kind of certificate at the end of the course. Most people undergo this training only for the certificate because it will come in handy for career development or for jumping jobs. The slender sarcasm in the last sentence is deliberate, because it is not always guaranteed that a certain course actually successfully enhanced a person's Soft Skills until and unless it is vigorously practiced.

The second way of acquiring Soft Skills is by self-training via books and is the most useful because an individual trains himself because he wants to get ahead in life. He knows that if he does not practice, he will be the one to be blamed for the failure. With the advent of the Internet, Soft Skills material can be found easily on the net. Of course, it goes without saying that you would have to filter some unnecessary things out as there is also a lot of unwanted information on the internet.

A sure shot way to train oneself in Soft Skills is to begin by socializing with friends, colleagues, peers and other members of the society. Start by engaging in small talk to improve communication skills in an informal way on topics like; language proficiency, listening, discussing, self-esteem, overcoming stage fear, body language, etiquette and manners etc. The list could be endless.

Even as you read this, educational institutions are changing their methodology and shifting to student-centric learning as the result of such a methodology is excellent. Many universities are embedding Soft Skill learning into their syllabi because it has added advantages. Students are encouraged to participate in a way that learning is enjoyed and are learning hard skills through Soft Skills. This becomes an ideal way of teaching and more knowledge is imparted in a short period of time. Moreover, it also helps you to improve discourse as the years pass by after a long period of time. To set things right, imbibing Soft Skills begins at the cradle. A lot of effort should be put by the parents to make sure that their children's personality is pleasing and habits are excellent. As the world is fast shrinking to become a global village, both parents have to work to meet the high standard of life as well as to pay the ever rising cost of education. Parents rarely have time to interact with their children let alone inculcate Soft Skills. Since the cost of the education is high, they expect the school to teach them the Soft Skills and schools, in turn pass the buck to colleges or centers of higher learning to equip them with the Soft Skills required. The end-case scenario is that everyone knows that they have to do it and nobody does it. The students are the sufferers in the process of the blame game. As soft skills are to be developed as intricate features of one's personality so must be included in the behavior of oneself.

ROLE OF EDUCATIONAL INSTITUTIONS FOR DEVELOPING SOFT SKILLS

The first step is for the educational institutions to recognize the needs of the students, gauge their weaknesses and then take steps to patch them up with the required training. They also need to raise the awareness of the students about the importance of Soft Skills and doing a SWOT analysis of each and every student. Specialists can be hired for this. Students should be encouraged to read books that are focused on improving Soft Skills, attend training courses, take part in debates and socialize with their peers. Each student should be encouraged to present a topic of their choice during the seminar sessions.

An addition to this, a period with a defined syllabus should be incorporated as a subject. At school level, students may be required to do a research and present a paper or a small write-up and submit the results during a particular period. At institutes of higher learning, a Soft Skill class can be arranged with topics like leadership skill, listening or writing skills, cross cultural conflict, problem solving can be introduced. Such practices are well received by student and it basically turns out to be fun learning for them.

Care must be taken because most colleges and universities overload students with subject's related to hard skills. It is an astonishing fact that most universities believe that the more subjects they teach, the better their students become and more are the chances of placements. Placements have become the driving force behind the choice of college/

university when choosing which college they should attend after school.

Universities and colleges that already have Soft Skill department have another issue. They believe that they do all the hard work in training the students to become achievers and the Communication and Soft Skills faculties takes away all the accolades after the student is placed. True interest regarding the future of the candidate in never displayed. This can be converted into a major scoring point with a little logical thinking in planning and application of courses. An elegant way of offering Soft Skills training is to embed in the teaching methodology of the technical faculty who teaches the subject i.e. hard skill course. This way, no changes need to be made to the program curriculum but the changes are reflected in the teaching methodology. An example would be a faculty who teaches, for example, Psychology. He should plan a lecture by determining what Soft Skills s/he wishes to enhance on that day, and then he should consider how the required subject content can be arranged to support this goal. Correctly applied, such an approach to teaching will automatically increase the attractiveness and effectiveness of a course regarding both, hard skills and Soft Skills.

Of course, it goes without saying that the faculty needs to be trained first in Soft Skills and them letting them choose the methodology and then practice it with the help of a Soft Skills trainer. In due course, it becomes a methodology that they automatically follow thereby increasing the Soft Skills of the students multifold.

In conclusion, we can say that Soft Skills occupy supreme importance and individuals who do not have them will soon be out of scenario. One has to take the trouble to acquire Soft

Skills beyond academic or technical knowledge. Soft Skills are gaining importance in all areas of the work industry. Faculties have a major role to play here by imparting their respective courses by using Soft Skills and at the same time making sure that their students practice Soft Skills during their University time. It is high time for the trainers, lecturers and faculties to change their methodology in imparting education. This holds true for schools, colleges, Universities as well as parents. It is everybody's responsibility to make sure that proper grooming, etiquette and Soft Skills are practiced at all times. This world would be a better place to live in. If each individual contributes his/her bit, the society, at large, would improve dramatically, thereby contributing to the peace of the world in a big way.

COMMUNICATION SKILLS

Communication is about more than just exchanging information. It's about understanding the emotion and intentions behind the information. Effective communication is also a two-way process. It's not only how you convey a message so that it is received and understood by someone in exactly the way you intended, it's also how you listen to gain the full meaning of what's being said and to make the other person feel heard and understood.

More than just the words you use, effective communication combines a set of skills including nonverbal communication, engaged listening, managing stress in the moment, the ability to communicate assertively, and the capacity to recognize and understand your own emotions and those of the person you are communicating with.

Effective communication is the glue that helps you–

deepen your connections to others and improve teamwork, decision making, and problem solving. It enables you to communicate even negative or difficult messages without creating conflict or destroying trust.

While effective communication is a learned skill, it is more effective when it's spontaneous rather than formulaic. A speech that is read, for example, rarely has the same impact as a speech that's delivered (or appears to be delivered) spontaneously. Of course, it takes time and effort to develop these skills and become an effective communicator. The more effort and practice you put in, the more instinctive and spontaneous your communication skills will become.

Steps for Improving Communication Skills

1. Become an engaged listener

People often focus on what they should say, but effective communication is less about talking and more about listening. Listening well means not just understanding the words or the information being communicated, but also understanding the emotions the speaker is trying to communicate.

There's a big difference between engaged listening and simply hearing. When you really listen—when you're engaged with what's being said—you'll hear the subtle intonations in someone's voice that tell you how that person is feeling and the emotions they're trying to communicate. When you're an engaged listener, not only will you better understand the other person, you'll also make that person feel heard and understood, which can help build a stronger, deeper connection between you.

By communicating in this way, you'll also experience a process that lowers stress and supports physical and emotional well-being. If the person you're talking to is calm, for example, listening in an engaged way will help to calm you, too. Similarly, if the person is agitated, you can help calm them by listening in an attentive way and making the person feel understood.

How do you Become an Engaged Listener?

If your goal is to fully understand and connect with the other person, listening in an engaged way will often come naturally. If it doesn't, try the following tips. The more you practice them, the more satisfying and rewarding your interactions with others will become.

- **Focus fully on the speaker,** his or her body language, tone of voice, and other nonverbal cues. Tone of voice conveys emotion, so if you're thinking about other things, checking text messages or doodling, you're almost certain to miss the nonverbal cues and the emotional content behind the words being spoken. And if the person talking is similarly distracted, you'll be able to quickly pick up on it. If you find it hard to concentrate on some speakers, try repeating their words over in your head—it'll reinforce their message and help you stay focused.
- **Favor your right ear.** The left side of the brain contains the primary processing centers for both speech comprehension and emotions. Since the left side of the brain is connected to the right side of the body, favoring your right ear can help you better detect the emotional nuances of what someone is saying. Try keeping your posture straight, your chin down, and tilting your right ear towards the speaker—this will

make it easier to pick up on the higher frequencies of human speech that contain the emotional content of what's being said.

- **Avoid interrupting or trying to redirect the conversation to your concerns,** by saying something like, "If you think that's bad, let me tell you what happened to me." Listening is not the same as waiting for your turn to talk. You can't concentrate on what someone's saying if you're forming what you're going to say next. Often, the speaker can read your facial expressions and know that your mind's elsewhere.
- **Show your interest in what's being said.** Nod occasionally, smile at the person, and make sure your posture is open and inviting. Encourage the speaker to continue with small verbal comments like "yes" or "uh huh."
- **Try to set aside judgment.** In order to communicate effectively with someone, you don't have to like them or agree with their ideas, values, or opinions. However, you do need to set aside your judgment and withhold blame and criticism in order to fully understand a person. The most difficult communication, when successfully executed, can lead to the most unlikely and profound connection with someone.
- **Provide feedback.** If there seems to be a disconnect, reflect what has been said by paraphrasing. "What I'm hearing is," or "Sounds like you are saying," are great ways to reflect back. Don't simply repeat what the speaker has said verbatim, though—you'll sound insincere or unintelligent. Instead, express what the speaker's words mean to you. Ask questions to clarify

certain points: "What do you mean when you say..." or "Is this what you mean?"

2. **Pay attention to nonverbal signals**

When we communicate things that we care about, we do so mainly using nonverbal signals. Nonverbal communication, or body language, includes facial expressions, body movement and gestures, eye contact, posture, the tone of your voice, and even your muscle tension and breathing. The way you look, listen, move, and react to another person tells them more about how you're feeling than words alone ever can.

Developing the ability to understand and use nonverbal communication can help you connect with others, express what you really mean, navigate challenging situations, and build better relationships at home and work.

- You can enhance effective communication by using open body language—arms uncrossed, standing with an open stance or sitting on the edge of your seat, and maintaining eye contact with the person you're talking to.
- You can also use body language to emphasize or enhance your verbal message—patting a friend on the back while complimenting him on his success, for example, or pounding your fists to underline your message.

Tips for improving how you read nonverbal communication

- **Be aware of individual differences.** People from different countries and cultures tend to use different nonverbal communication gestures, so it's important to take age, culture, religion, gender, and emotional state into account when reading body language signals.

- **Look at nonverbal communication signals as a group.** Don't read too much into a single gesture or nonverbal cue. Consider all of the nonverbal signals you receive, from eye contact to tone of voice to body language. Anyone can slip up occasionally and let eye contact slip, for example, or briefly cross their arms without meaning to. Consider the signals as a whole to get a better "read" on a person.

Tips for improving how you deliver nonverbal communication

- **Use nonverbal signals that match up with your words.** Nonverbal communication should reinforce what is being said, not contradict it. If you say one thing, but your body language says something else, your listener will likely feel you're being dishonest. For example, you can't say "yes" while shaking your head no.
- **Adjust your nonverbal signals according to the context.** The tone of your voice, for example, should be different when you're addressing a child than when you're addressing a group of adults. Similarly, take into account the emotional state and cultural background of the person you're interacting with.
- **Use body language to convey positive feelings** even when you're not actually experiencing them. If you're nervous about a situation—a job interview, important presentation, or first date, for example—you can use positive body language to signal confidence, even

though you're not feeling it. Instead of tentatively entering a room with your head down, eyes averted, and sliding into a chair, try standing tall with your shoulders back, smiling and maintaining eye contact, and delivering a firm handshake. It will make you feel more self-confident and help to put the other person at ease.

3. Keep stress in check

To communicate effectively, you need to be aware of and in control of your emotions. And that means learning how to manage stress. When you're stressed, you're more likely to misread other people, send confusing or off-putting nonverbal signals, and lapse into unhealthy knee-jerk patterns of behavior.

How many times have you felt stressed during a disagreement with your spouse, kids, boss, friends, or coworkers and then said or done something you later regretted? If you can quickly relieve stress and return to a calm state, you'll not only avoid such regrets, but in many cases you'll also help to calm the other person as well. It's only when you're in a calm, relaxed state that you'll be able to know whether the situation requires a response, or whether the other person's signals indicate it would be better to remain silent.

Staying calm under pressure

In situations such as a job interview, business presentation, high-pressure meeting, or introduction to a loved one's family, for example, it's important to manage your emotions, think on your feet, and effectively communicate under pressure. These tips can help:

- **Use stalling tactics** to give yourself time to think. Have a question repeated, or ask for clarification of a statement before responding.
- **Pause to collect your thoughts.** Silence isn't necessarily a bad thing—pausing can make you seem more in control than rushing your response.
- **Make one point** and provide an example or supporting piece of information. If your response is too long or you waffle about a number of points, you risk losing the listener's interest. Follow one point with an example and then gauge the listener's reaction to tell if you should make a second point.
- **Deliver your words clearly.** In many cases, how you say something can be as important as what you say. Speak clearly, maintain an even tone, and make eye contact. Keep your body language relaxed and open.
- **Wrap up with a summary** and then stop. Summarize your response and then stop talking, even if it leaves a silence in the room. You don't have to fill the silence by continuing to talk.

Quick stress relief technique for effective communication

When things start to get heated in the middle of a conversation, you need something quick and immediate to bring down the emotional intensity. By learning to quickly reduce stress in the moment, though, you can safely face any strong emotions you're experiencing, regulate your feelings, and behave appropriately. When you know how to maintain a relaxed, energized state of awareness—even when something upsetting happens—you can remain emotionally available and engaged.

To deal with stress during communication:

- **Recognize when you're becoming stressed.** Your body will let you know if you're stressed as you communicate. Are your muscles or your stomach tight and/or sore? Are your hands clenched? Is your breath shallow? Are you "forgetting" to breathe?
- **Take a moment to calm down** before deciding to continue a conversation or postpone it.
- **Bring your senses to the rescue** and quickly manage stress by taking a few deep breaths, clenching and relaxing muscles, or recalling a soothing, sensory-rich image, for example. The best way to rapidly and reliably relieve stress is through the senses: sight, sound, touch, taste, and smell. But each person responds differently to sensory input, so you need to find things that are soothing to you.
- **Look for humor in the situation.** When used appropriately, humor is a great way to relieve stress when communicating. When you or those around you start taking things too seriously, find a way to lighten the mood by sharing a joke or amusing story.
- **Be willing to compromise.** Sometimes, if you can both bend a little, you'll be able to find a happy middle ground that reduces the stress levels for everyone concerned. If you realize that the other person cares much more about something than you do, compromise may be easier for you and a good investment in the future of the relationship.
- **Agree to disagree,** if necessary, and take time away from the situation so everyone can calm down. Take a

quick break and move away from the situation. Go for a stroll outside if possible, or spend a few minutes meditating. Physical movement or finding a quiet place to regain your balance can quickly reduce stress.

4. **Assert yourself**

Direct, assertive expression makes for clear communication and can help boost self-esteem and decision-making. Being assertive means expressing your thoughts, feelings, and needs in an open and honest way, while standing up for yourself and respecting others. It does NOT mean being hostile, aggressive, or demanding. Effective communication is always about understanding the other person, not about winning an argument or forcing your opinions on others.

To improve assertiveness:

- **Value yourself and your opinions.** They are as important as anyone else's.
- **Know your needs and wants.** Learn to express them without infringing on the rights of others.
- **Express negative thoughts** in a positive way. It's OK to be angry, but you must be respectful as well.
- **Receive feedback positively.** Accept compliments graciously, learn from your mistakes, ask for help when needed.
- **Learn to say "no."** Know your limits and don't let others take advantage of you. Look for alternatives so everyone feels good about the outcome.

BARRIERS TO EFFECTIVE INTERPERSONAL COMMUNICATION

- **Stress and out-of-control emotion.** When you're stressed or emotionally overwhelmed, you're more likely to misread other people, send confusing or off-putting nonverbal signals, and lapse into unhealthy knee-jerk patterns of behavior. Take a moment to calm down before continuing a conversation.
- **Lack of focus.** You can't communicate effectively when you're multitasking. If you're planning what you're going to say next, daydreaming, checking text messages, or thinking about something else, you're almost certain to miss nonverbal cues in the conversation. You need to stay focused on the moment-to-moment experience.
- **Inconsistent body language.** Nonverbal communication should reinforce what is being said, not contradict it. If you say one thing, but your body language says something else, your listener will likely feel you're being dishonest. For example, you can't say "yes" while shaking your head no.
- **Negative body language.** If you disagree with or dislike what's being said, you may use negative body language to rebuff the other person's message, such as crossing your arms, avoiding eye contact, or tapping your feet. You don't have to agree, or even like what's being said, but to communicate effectively without making the other person defensive, it's important to avoid sending negative signals.

****

Unit II
Peace, Progress and Harmony

Chapter - 6

Locus of Control

MEANING AND CONCEPT OF LOCUS OF CONTROL

Control can be defined as the power to determine outcomes by directly influencing actions, people and events.

The word 'control' becomes more interesting when we have the word locus, before it. So locus is defined as a position, point or place, or more specifically, a location where something occurs.

So "Locus of Control is a belief about whether the outcomes of our action are contingent on what we do or on events outside our personal control."

According to Zimbardo "Locus of control is our behavior that is controlled by reward and punishment, and it is consequences for our actions that determine our beliefs about the causes of the actions." and our belief about what causes our actions, influence our behavior and attitude. According to JULIAN Rotter It is of two types:

1. Internal Locus of Control
2. External Locus of Control

Internal Locus of Control

People who base their success on their own work and believe that they control their life themselves, have an internal locus of control.

For example, if you're a person with an internal locus of control and you get a promotion at work or achieve some other type of success. It means your success was a direct result of your own hard work. So we can say internally locus people are hard on themselves, and they constantly analyze what they did wrong.

Characteristics of people having Internal Locus of Control:

1. They are more likely to take responsibilities for their actions.
2. They are less influenced by the opinions of other people.
3. They often do better task, when they are allowed to work at their own pace.
4. They have a strong sense of self-efficacy.
5. They tend to work hard to achieve the things they want.
6. They feel confident while facing challenges.
7. They are happier and more independent.
8. They achieve greater success at the work place.

External Locus of Control

People who have an external locus of control, they might attribute that promotion or success to external environmental factors such as luck, fate or some type of divine intervention.

Let's take an example if you were denied a promotion then your locus of control is internal, you would find a way to blame yourself for the perceived failure. If your locus of control is external, it would be easy to blame outside sources beyond your control.

Externally locus people look at everything around them as a part of success or failure; they always praise those around them for well done even they had nothing to do with it.

Characteristics of the people having External Locus of Control

1. They blame outside forces for their circumstances.
2. They credit luck for any success.
3. They don't believe that they can change their situation through their own efforts.
4. They feel hopeless in difficult situations.

****

Chapter - 7

Stress and its Management

STRESS

Stress is body's way of responding to any kind of demand. It can be caused by both good and bad experience. When people feel stressed by something going on around them, their bodies react by releasing chemicals into the blood. These chemicals give people more energy and strength, which can be a good thing if their stress is caused by physical danger. But this can also be a bad, if their stress is due to emotions and there is no outlet for extra energy and strength.

Stress is a generally applied to various psychological and physiological pressures experienced or felt by people throughout their lives.

So Stress is defined as "a state of psychological and physiological imbalance resulting from the disparity between situational demand and the individual's ability and motivation to meet those needs."

According to Dr. Hans Selye– Stress is the rate of all wear and tear caused by life.

Stress can be positive or negative also.

CAUSE OR SOURCE OF STRESS

General Causes of Stress are given as

1. **Survival Stress**– This stress is common in all people and animals. When we are afraid from someone or someone may physically hurt us, our body naturally responds with a burst of energy so we will be better able to survive the dangerous situation. This type of stress is called as a survival stress.
2. **Internal Stress**– Internal stresses occur when people make themselves stressed. This happens when we worry about things that we can't control or put ourselves in situations which will cause stress. Some people become addicted to the kind of hurried, tense, lifestyle that results from being under stress, they always look for stressful situation and feel stress about thing that are not stressful.
3. **Environmental Stress**– This is a response around us that cause stress, such as noise, crowding and pressure from work or family. Identifying these environmental stresses and learning to avoid them that will help to lower your stress.
4. **Fatigue and Overwork**– It can be caused by working too much or too hard at your job, school, or home. It can also be caused by not knowing how to manage your time well or how to take time out for rest and relaxation. This can be hardest kinds of stress to avoid because many people feel this is out of their control.
5. **Civic Amenities**– Poor civic amenities in the area in which we lives like Inadequate or lack of public facilities like improper water supply, excessive noise or air

pollution, lack of proper transport facility can also cause stress.

6. **Life Changes**– Life changes can bring stress to a person like getting older and abrupt life changes include death or accident of a loved one person can cause the stress.
7. **Frustration**– Frustration is another cause of stress which arises when goal-directed behavior gets blocked. This type of stress can be reduced by removing the barrier and help them to reach their goals.
8. **Racial, Caste, and Religious Conflicts**– people living in areas, where people based on differences seen in their race, caste and religion do suffer from more stress.
9. **Technological Changes**– When there is any change in technical fields, people feel the constant fear of losing jobs or need to adjust to new technologies can cause the stress.
10. **Career Changes**– When a person suddenly joins another job, he is under stress to shoulder new responsibilities adequately. Under promotion, over-promotion, demotion and transfers can also cause stress.

Causes of Stress at work place

1. **Career Concern**: If an employee is very much behind in the corporate ladder, then he feels stress. If he seems that there is no opportunity for self-growth, he may feel stress. Hence, unfulfilled career expectations are the source of stress.
2. **Role Ambiguity**: It occurs when the person doesn't know his tasks and responsibilities clearly. It creates confusion in the minds of the worker and causes stress.

3. **Rotating Work Shifts**: Stress may occur in individuals who work on different shifts. Employees want to do work on day shift for some days and then on the night shift. This may create problems in adjusting to the shift timings, and can affect not only personal life but also family life of the employee.

4. **Role Conflict**: It takes place when people have different expectation or when a job demands a certain type of behavior that is against the person's moral values.

5. **Work Overload**: Excessive workload cause stress as it puts a person under tremendous pressure.

6. **Work Under Load**: Doing less work or jobs of routine nature would lead to monotony and boredom, which can also cause stress.

7. **Poor Working Condition**: Employees may be subject to poor working conditions like bad lighting and ventilation, unhygienic sanitation facilities, excessive noise, dust, presence of toxic gases and fumes, inadequate safety measures etc. all these conditions create physiological and psychological imbalance in human's life thereby causing stress.

8. **Lack of Group Cohesiveness**: Every group is characterized by its cohesiveness, although they differ in its degree. Individuals feel stress when there is no unity among work group members. There is mistrust, jealousy, frequent quarrels, etc. in groups and this also cause stress to employees.

9. **Interpersonal and Intergroup Conflict**: These conflicts take place due to differences in perceptions, attitudes, values and beliefs between two or more individuals and

groups. Such conflicts may also cause stress for group members.

10. **Organizational Changes**: When organizational changes occur, people have to adapt these changes, and this may lead to stress. Stress is higher when changes are unusual like transfer or adoption of new technology.

11. **Lack of Social Support**: When individuals believe that they have friends and social support of others at work place, their ability to cope with the effects of stress increases. If this kind of social support is not available, then a person feels more stress.

TYPE OF STRESS

Generally stress is of three types which are given as:

1. Acute Stress
2. Episodic Stress
3. Chronic Stress

1. Acute Stress

Acute stress is the most widely experienced stress caused by the daily demands and pressures of the near future. It is due to the excitement, joy and thrill in our lives e.g. Riding a roller coaster in a theme park, is a situation that brings about acute stress, yet brings excitement. We feel the effects of acute stress, such as vomiting, tension headaches, and other psychological and physiological symptoms. An acute stress occurs for a very short period of time, the symptoms come out when the stress has already accumulated and the symptoms of the acute stress are given as:

- Emotional distress such as anger, anxiety, irritability and acute periods of depression
- Physical problems such as headache, pain, stomach upset, dizziness, heart palpitations, shortness of breath, hypertension and bowel disorders.

2. Episodic Stress

When acute stress occurs too frequently then it is called episodic stress. This type of stress is usually seen in people who make self-inflicted, unrealistic or demands which get all clamored up and bring too much stress to accomplish these goals. Episodic stress is not like chronic stress because this type of stress occurs from time to time yet not as frequently as acute stress does.

Episodic stress is also observed in people with "Type A" personality, which involves being over competitive, aggressive, demanding and sometimes tense and hostile. The symptoms of episodic stress are given as;

- Longer periods of depression, anxiety disorders and emotional distress
- Ceaseless worrying
- Persistent physical symptoms similar to those found in acute stress
- Coronary heart diseases, or other heart problems

3. Chronic Stress

Chronic stress is totally opposite of acute stress; it's not exciting and thrilling, but dangerous and unhealthy. Chronic stress tears the life of a person apart his mind, body or spirit.

This type of stress is brought by long exposure to stressors, such as unhappy marriage, traumatic experiences,

unwanted career, and stress of poverty, chronic illnesses, relationship conflicts, political problems, and dysfunctional families. These stressful situations seem to be unending, it can be life-threatening, lead a person to resort to violence, suicide and self-harm. Serious illnesses like, heart attack, cancer, and psychological problems such as clinical depression can also originate from chronic stress.
Symptoms of chronic stress are given as:

- Dry mouth
- Difficulty in breathing
- Pounding heart
- Stomach ache
- Headache
- Diaphoresis
- Frequent urination
- Tightening of muscles
- ….and more…

Mental symptoms of chronic stress given are:

- Sudden irritability
- Tension
- Problems with concentration
- Difficulty in sleeping
- Narrowed perception
- Frequent feelings of fatigue

STRESS MANAGEMENT

Stress is a normal part of life which affects your physical and mental health. Chronic stress can increase your risk for gastric ulcers, osteoporosis, and sexual dysfunction. It is linked to other physical illness including hypertension, heart disease, diabetes, asthma, and arthritis. Chronic stress can also affect the immune system, leading to an increase in infections and worsening of skin conditions such as eczema, and mood disorders, as well as anxiety.

Stress has a detrimental effect on memory and cognition. It is often associated with deficits in learning ability. It could cause psychiatric disorders such as depression and anxiety.

The efforts to control, reduce, or learn to tolerate the threats that leads to stress are called stress management or coping.

Stress management is a technique intended to equip a person with effective coping mechanisms for dealing with psychological stress. It includes calm, clear thoughts and confidence in yourself and your ability to accomplish the goals set for yourself.

Stress management can be defined as interventions designed to reduce the impact of stressors. It might include different approaches to help you better deal with stress adversity like problem-solving, prioritization and time management. Another approach is to practice relaxing techniques such as deep breathings, yoga, meditation, tai chi, exercise and prayer. Improving personal relationships is an important component of stress management.

Stress Management can be Divided into two Categories:

1. Emotion focused stress management or coping—In emotion-focused coping, people try to manage their emotions in the face of stress, seeking to change the way they feel about or perceive a problem. E.g. it includes strategies such as accepting sympathy from others and looking at the bright side of a situation.
2. Problem-focused management—Problem-focused management attempts to modify the stressful problem or source of stress. Problem–focused strategies lead to change in behavior to deal with stress. E.g. A group study improves poor classroom performance is an example of problem-focused management.

Techniques of Stress Management are given as

1. Stress management seminars-The stress management seminars can help you to develop skills to manage and prevent excessive and chronicle stress. This type of programmes promotes a holistic approach that addresses body, mind and spirit which help us to:
    1. Identify the actual causes of your stress.
    2. Learn new techniques which help you prevent harmful stresses from occurring.
    3. Improve your mood and your stress resilience. You will be able to successfully manage your stress at work and in your personal life.
    4. Improve your life quality professionally, personally, and socially.

5. Use mindfulness to improve your life quality and ability to manage stress.
6. Adopt healthy habits that enhance management skills, and help to lead a happier life.
7. Learn how to address your issues more effectively and also learn to manage your daily life smoothly.
8. Turn your personal difficulties into opportunities and stressful situations into a joy.
9. Learn how to manage stress without affecting your ability to achieve your goals.

2. Acupuncture– In acupressure the fine needles are inserted in the skin at key points in your body to boost your body's natural painkillers and increase blood circulation to reduce the stress.
3. Counseling– Counseling is given to develop coping skills that address feelings, illnesses and challenging situation.
4. Deep breathing– Breathing from diaphragm is taken to establish a pattern of slower, deeper and more efficient breathing to reduce stress.
5. Visualization– Pictorial images of relaxing places and situations also helpful to cope with negative emotions, feelings and circumstances.
6. Massage therapy– It involve pressing and rubbing the body's soft tissues-muscle, connective tissue, tendons, ligaments and skin-for comfort, healing and pain reduction.
7. Meditation– The meditation practice focuses the mind, tuning out distractions, and also involves repeating a word or phrase, or visualizing a peaceful place which is helpful

in reducing the stress.

8. Mindfulness– A technique in which we focused, engaged and completely absorbed in the present moment also reduces stress.
9. Progressive muscle relaxation– It is used for tensing and relaxing the muscle throughout our body to reduce the muscle tension and calm the anxious feelings.
10. Resilience training– Learning to balance the demands with your available resources; controlling the controllable; and seeing life's situation as challenges or opportunities rather than overwhelming obstacles.
11. Yoga– Various types of mind-body practices that combine a series of precise postures with controlled breathing which help us in relaxing your mind and increase strength and flexibility.

Some other Techniques of Stress Management are given as:

- Self-understanding
- Self-management
- Conflict resolution
- Adopting a more positive attitude
- Self-talk
- Breathing exercises
- Meditation
- Exercise
- Altering your diet
- Taking more regular and effective rest

- Becoming more organized and reducing the generation of clutter
- Setting priorities can help to reduce anxiety
- Effective stress management involves learning to set limits and to say "No" to some demands that others make.
- We can never eliminate stress from our lives as stressful situations are part of our life. However, we can learn to react to stress in a positive manner and take control of the situation rather than allowing the stress to remain in control.

Following Habits can help to Relieve Stress:

1. Regular meditation,
2. Physical exercise,
3. Balanced diet,
4. Focused thinking,
5. Control of anger,
6. Managing depression,
7. Maintaining calmness in stressful situations,
8. Having a positive attitude towards life,
9. Harmony towards self and others, etc.

General Suggestions to Manage the Stress are given as:

1. Turn threat into challenge– When a stressful situation might be controllable, the best coping strategy is to treat the situation as challenge, focusing on ways to control

it. e.g. if you experience stress because your car is breaking down, you might take a course in auto mechanics and learn to deal directly with the car's problems.

2. Making a threatening situation less threatening– When a stressful situation seems to be uncontrollable, a different approach must be taken. It is possible to change one's appraisal of the situation, modifying one's attitude towards it.

3. Change your goal– When one is faced with an uncontrollable situation, a reasonable strategy is to adopt new goal. E.g. a dancer who has been lost her legs may no longer aspire to a career in dance but might modify her goals and try to become a dance instructor.

4. Prepare for stress before it happens– A final strategy for coping with stress is proactive coping, anticipating and preparing for stress before it is encounter, through proactive coping people can ready themselves for upcoming stressful events and thereby reduce their consequences. E.g. if you are expecting to go through a number of exam in week, you can try to arrange your schedule so you have more time to study.

****

Chapter - 8

Social Interaction and Social Influence

MEANING OF SOCIAL INFLUENCE

Social influence occurs when one's emotions, opinions, or behaviors are affected by others. It takes in many forms and can be seen in conformity, socialization, peer pressure, leadership. According to Harvard it is of three types

1. **Compliance**– It occurs when people appear to agree with others, but actually keep their dissenting opinions private.
2. **Identification**– Identification means people are influenced by someone who is respected, such as a famous celebrity.
3. **Internalization**– It takes place when people accept a belief or behavior and agree with both publically and privately.

According to Morton Deutsch and Harold Gerard Social Influence is of Two Types:

1. Informational social influence
2. Normative social influence

    1. Informational social influence is an influence to accept information from another as evidence about reality. It

comes into play when people are uncertain, either because stimuli are intrinsically ambiguous or because there is social disagreement.

2. Normative influence is an influence to conform to the positive expectations of others. It leads to public compliance, whereas informational influence leads to private acceptance.

ASPECTS OF SOCIAL INFLUENCE

1. Social influence changes the attitudes or behavior in order to adhere to existing social norms.
2. Social influence involves direct request from one person to another.
3. Social influence in which one person obeys direct orders from another to perform some duties.

Social influence occurs when other people have an effect on behavior such as peer pressure. In simple words, peer pressure means being pushed over by friends to do something which you would not do otherwise. It affects your thinking and it may alter your decisions. Social Influence can have positive or negative effects on people. Not all social influence is negative. Not all peer pressure is negative. Peer pressure starts at the Adolescence stage when they try to create an identity for themselves. They have a desperate need to belong to a group and becoming a soft target for peer pressure. Bad advice, curiosity to try something that everyone else is indulging in or just the fear of being teased by friends (for not doing what others are doing) lead teens to do things they would rather not do, if left to their better judgment. His behavior as well as his perception about life depends much on how these peers affect him. At this adolescence stage peer relations become the core of a person's life and they want to socialize as much as they can and have fun with their peers, rather than spending time with their families. They seem to prefer their friends and classmates for close relations. The result is that there are frequent conflicts and disagreements between teens and their parents. They tend to maintain distance from their parents and eventually, lose all the emotional closeness and warmth that was once there between them.

SOCIAL INTERACTION

Man is a social animal. It is difficult for him to live in isolation. They always live in groups. Their behavior is mutually affected as we know. When two persons talk with each other or respond to each other on telephone or internet, develop correspondence through letter, there is an interaction. e.g. A mother suckling milk to her child, there is interaction between mother and her child. A doctor attends a patient, there is interaction between a doctor and patient, a customer buys a thing from a shopkeeper, there is a interaction between a shopkeeper and a customer. When a passenger gets ticket from the booking clerk there is an interaction between clerk and passenger. It means interaction is a social relationship among the individuals. It is a sort of action and reaction among the people.

Social life is not possible without interaction. So Social interaction are reciprocal relationship which influence the interacting individuals but also the quality of relationship

According to Erving Goffmen "Social interaction is the process by which we act and react to those around us. It also includes those acts which people perform towards each other and the responses they give in return".

According to Merrill "Social interaction is the general process whereby two or more persons are in a meaningful contact, as a result of which their behavior is modified slightly".

According to Corkiness "Social interaction is a process which influences the overt behavior or state of mind of the individuals".

Social interaction is an event which changes the behavior and attitude ofthe interacting persons. It is a social relationship among persons which changes the societal conditions of life of the people. Interaction is the soul of social life and relationship. It produces group which is the foundation stone of society.

Social interaction has two conditions Social Contact and Communication:

1. Social contact is the first phase of interaction and they are always established through the medium of someone.
2. Communication may be the form of direct interaction through person to person or it may take place through some medium such as telephone, telegraph, television etc.

FORMS OF SOCIAL INTERACTION IN A SOCIETY

It is found in various forms among human societies which are given as:

1. **Between individual and individual–** It is the interaction between at least two persons e.g. Interaction between the

doctor and the patient, the mother and the child, the customer and the shopkeeper etc.

2. **Between individual and group**– It is the interaction between one person and group of people. A teacher teaching his class, a speaker addressing the audience, an Imam leading prayers are its common examples.

3. **Between group and group**– This is found between two groups of people like two teams playing match, two forces fighting against each other, two delegates discussing an issue.

4. **Between individuals and culture**– This form is found when the people listen to radio, see television, read newspaper, enjoy pictures and observe exhibitions. Films, exhibitions, theatre, drama, circus, fairs and other socio-cultural activities are included in the Culture of the society. People have social interaction and social relationship with these media of mass communication and get social change in their life. The people change these media as they require on the other hand. In this way reciprocal process between the people and the culture goes on.

TYPE OF SOCIAL INTERACTION

According to Young and Mack social interaction is of two types–

1. **Direct or Physical interaction**– It involves physical action among the individuals. Beating, biting, thrashing, pulling, pushing, killing, scratching, boxing, wrestling, kissing etc. are the examples of direct interaction. Two teams playing match and a war between the forces of two countries are also examples of this interaction.

2. **Symbolic Interaction**– There are different types of relationships between people. It involves the use of language and symbols. It means communication through a common language is symbolic process. This is the most common method of interaction in human societies. Human beings convey their ideas through language and it is completed by reciprocal response. All cultures develop, expand and change only through language symbolic interaction. Without language no culture can be alive. Through language man stores its previous experiences and transmits them to the next generation with a change.

Man uses instruments to facilitate this like telephone, wireless, telegraph, postal system, rail road, sea and air services all are various means of communication and transportation. Gestures are also symbolic ones. Deaf and dumb convey their ideas through voice, and gestures of hands and eyes.

Social interaction is mainly divided into four categories which are given as:

1. Competition
2. Cooperation
3. Accommodation
4. Assimilation.

1. Competition

Competition is one of the dissociative forms of social processes. It occurs when there is an insufficient supply of anything that human beings desire and in sufficient in the sense that all cannot have as much of it as they wish.

The people also compete for power, name, fame, glory, status, money, luxuries and other things which are not easily available. Since scarcity is in a sense of inevitable condition of social life, competition of some sort or the other is found in all the societies. For example, there are normally more people who want jobs than which are available; hence there is competition for them. Among those who are already employed, there is likewise competition for better jobs. Thus there is competition not only for bread but also for luxuries, power, social positions, name and fame and all other things not in approach..

According to Sutherland, Woodword and Maxwell "Competition is an impersonal, unconscious, continuous straggle between individuals and groups for satisfaction which, because of their limited supply, all may not have".

According to E.S. Bogardus "Competition is a contest to obtain something which does not exist in quantity sufficient to meet the demand."

According to Biesanz and Biesanz, "Competition is the striving of two or more persons for the same goal with is limited so that all cannot share it".

According to Park and Burgess "Competition is an interaction without social contract".

So competition is a process by which two or more people attempt to achieve a goal that only one can attain. It is a positive thing that can motivate people to achieve goals. However, competition can also lead to psychological stress, a lack of cooperation in social relationships, inequality and even cause conflict.

Characteristics of Competition

(i) It is Universal

Competition is found in every society and in every age. It is found in every group. It is universal not only is human society but also in the plant and animal worlds. It is the natural result of the universal struggle for existence.

(ii) It is Impersonal

Competition is not a personal action. It is an 'interaction without social contact." The competitors are not in contact and do not know one another. They do not compete with each other on a personal level. The attention of all the competitors is fixed on the goal or the reward they aim at. Due to this reason competition is known as an impersonal affair.

(iii) It is an Unconscious Activity

Competition takes place at the unconscious level. Achievement of goal or the reward is regarded as the main object of competitors. For example, the students of a particular class get engaged to secure the highest marks in the final-examination. They do not conceive of their classmates as competitors. Students may, no doubt, be conscious about the competition but much concerned about marks.

Their attention is focused on the reward or goals rather on the competitors. It is a continuous process and never comes to an end.

Type of Competition

Competition can be divided into many categories which are given as:

1. Economic Competition

Economic competition is found in the field of economic activities like in the field of production, consumption, distribution and exchange of wealth. Competition between two industrial sectors for the production of goods is the example of economic competition

2. Cultural Competition

Cultural competition is found among different cultures. It occurs when two or more cultures try to establish their superiority over others. This type of competition leads to cultural diversities in society. When one culture tries to establish its supremacy over other cultures, it gives birth to cultural competition.

1. *Social Competition*

   Social competition is mainly found in modern societies for acquiring a high status, popularity, name and fame in society. Social competition plays a vital role in the determination of individual's status in society.

2. *Racial Competition*

   Racial competition is found among different races of the world. It takes place when one race tries to establish its superiority over the other. The whole human society is divided into a number of races and there always arises an intense competition among them. Similarly, in South Africa, there is a competition between the white and black races.

3. *Political Competition*

   Political competition takes place in the political field. In all democratic countries, competition is inevitable among the various political parties and even between the different members of a political party to obtain political power.

Type of competition –it is generally divided into two types

1. Personal Competition

In this competition, the competitors are well known to each other personally. Competition between the two students in class-room or competition between two players in a particular game is the bright example of personal competition.

2. Impersonal Competition

Impersonal competition takes place among the groups not among the individuals. In this competition, the competitors compete with one another not on personal level but as members of groups such as business, social and cultural groups. e.g. Competition between the various religious groups likes Hindus, Muslims, Christian, and Sikhs etc.

Role of Competition

Competition is considered to be very healthy and a necessary social process. It is indispensable in social life. It performs both positive and negative functions.

Positive role of competition is given as:

1. *Assignment of Right Individual at Right Place*

   Competition assigns right individual at right place in the social system. It provides the individuals better opportunities to satisfy their desires for new experiences and recognition at right time. It believes in achieved status. Competition determines who is to perform what function. The division of labor and specialization of function and work in modern life are the products of competition.

2. *Source of Motivation*

   Competition motivates other to excel or to obtain recognition or to win an award. The practice of awarding prizes and scholarships to those who occupy the few top position on the merit is designed to foster creativity and promote striving excellence. Competition stimulates achievement by lifting the levels of aspiration for which some individuals work harder for success.

3. *Conducive to Progress*

   Healthy and fair competition is considered essential for economic, social as well as technological and scientific progress. When a proper man is in the proper place the technological and general progress of the society cannot be hampered. People make their best efforts when they find themselves in competition. It is competition which has made inventions and discoveries in different possible Fields.

Negative Role of the competition is given as:

1. *Competition may Lead to Frustration*

   Competition may create emotional disturbances. It may develop unfriendly and unfavorable attitudes among the persons or groups toward one another. It may lead to neurosis through frustration and to violation of the rules by those who fail in the struggle for status according to "the rules of the game".

2. *Competition may Lead to Monopoly*

   Unlimited competition in a capitalist economy gives rise to monopoly. It throws the real needs of the people into waste and causes starvation in the midst of plenty. It may cause fear, insecurity and instability.

3. *Competition may lead to Conflict*

   Competition, if it is uncontrolled, may lead to conflicts. Sometimes it may become violent involving unethical and unfair means to divert the competitors' attention.

2. Cooperation

The term 'cooperation' has been derived from two Latin words – 'Co' meaning 'together' and Operation meaning 'to work'. Hence, cooperation means when two or more persons work together for the achievement of a common goal is called cooperation.

So Cooperation is a social process that gets things done; no group can complete its tasks or achieve its goals without cooperation from its members. Sometimes, cooperation work together with other forms of interaction, such as competition. For example, in a baseball game, a team plays together to achieve a victory

According to Merrill and Aldridge, "Cooperation is a form of social interaction where two or more persons work together to gain a common end".

According to Fairchild– Cooperation is the process by which the individuals or groups combine their effort in a more or less organized way for the attainment of common objective.

Co operation involves two elements common end and organized effort.

In cooperation when different persons have the same goals and also realize that individually they cannot achieve their goals, they work jointly for the fulfillment of goals.

Characteristics of cooperation are given as

1. It is an associative process of social interaction which takes place between two or more individuals or groups.
2. It is a conscious process in which individuals or groups have to work consciously.
3. It is a personal process in which individuals and groups personally meet and work together for a common objective.
4. It is a continuous process and there is continuity in the collective efforts in cooperation.
5. It is a universal process which is found in all groups, societies and nations.
6. It is a based upon two elements such as common end and organized effort.

At end we can say it is necessary for the progress of individual as well as society.

Types of Cooperation:

Cooperation is of two types. (i) Direct Cooperation (ii) Indirect Cooperation.

1. Direct Cooperation

It includes all those activities in which people do like things together. For example, playing together, working together, carrying a load together or pulling the car out of mud together. The essential character of this kind of cooperation is that people do such identical function which they can also do separately. This type of cooperation is voluntary e.g., cooperation between husband and wife, teacher and student, master and servant etc.

2. *Indirect Cooperation*

   It includes those activities in which people do unlike tasks together towards a common end. e.g. example when carpenters, plumbers and masons cooperate to build a house. This cooperation is based on the principle of the division of labor.

   In it people perform different functions but for the attainment of the common objective.

According to A.W. Green cooperation is of three type (1) Primary cooperation (ii) Secondary cooperation (iii) Tertiary cooperation.

1. *Primary Cooperation*

   This type of cooperation is found in primary groups such as in the family. In this form, there is an identification of interests between the individuals and the group. The achievement of the group includes the realization of the individual's interests.

2. *Secondary Cooperation*

   Secondary cooperation is found in secondary groups such as Government, industry, trade union and church etc. For example, in an industry, each may work in cooperation with others for his own wages, salaries, promotion, and profit and in some cases prestige and power. In this form of cooperation there is disparity of interests between the individuals.

3. *Tertiary Cooperation*

   This type of cooperation is found between the various big and small groups to meet a particular situation. In it, the attitudes of the cooperating parties are purely opportunistic; the organization of their cooperation is both loose and fragile. For example, two political parties with different ideologies may get united to defeat their rival party in an election.

According to Ogburn and Nimikoff Cooperation is of three types:

1. *General Cooperation*

   When some people cooperate for the common goals then it is known as general cooperation e.g. cooperation found in cultural functions is the general cooperation.

2. *Friendly Cooperation*

   When we want to attain the happiness and contentment of our group we give cooperation to each other, then this type of cooperation is known friendly cooperation e.g. dancing, singing, dating etc.

3. *Helping Cooperation*

   When some people work for the victims of famine or flood then this type of cooperation is known as helping cooperation.

Role of Cooperation

Cooperation is the most elementary form of social process without which society cannot exist. According to Kropotkin, it is so important in the life of an individual without it, difficult to survive. Even among the lowest animals such as ants and termites, cooperation is evident for survival. Cooperation is the foundation of our social life. The continuation of the human race requires the cooperation of male and female for reproduction and upbringing of children. Cooperation is social and psychological necessity of human life. It is needed at every step in our life. If one does not cooperate with others, he is left to live a solitary life. It is very difficult for a man to lead a happily conjugal life without the active cooperation of his wife and via-versa.

It is not only needed among the individuals and groups but also among the nations. It provides solutions for many international problems and disputes. The outstanding progress in science and technology, agriculture and industry, transport and communication would not have been possible without Cooperation

3. Accommodation

Adjustment is the way to life. It can take place in two ways such as adaptation and accommodation. Adaptation refers to the process of biological adjustment. Accommodation, on the other hand, implies the process of social adjustment. "Accommodation is the achievement of adjustment between people that permits harmonious efforts together in social situation." It is achieved by an individual through the acquisition of behavior patterns, habits and attitudes which are transmitted to him socially.

Thus, accommodation means adjusting oneself to the new environment.

According to Maclver and Page "The accommodation refers particularly to the process in which man attains sense of harmony with his environment".

According to Ogburn and Nimkoff, "Accommodation is a term used by sociologist to describe the adjustment to hostile individuals or groups."

According to Horton and Hunt defines "Accommodation is a process of developing temporary working agreements between conflicting individuals or groups".

Characteristic of accommodation are given as

1. *It is the End-result of Conflict*

   The involvement of individuals or groups in conflict makes them realize the importance of accommodation. Since conflict cannot take place continuously, they make room for accommodation. It is the natural result of conflict. If there were no conflict, there would be no need of accommodation.

2. *It is both Conscious and Unconscious Process*

   Accommodation is mainly an unconscious activity because a newborn individual accommodates himself with his family, caste, play-group, school, and neighborhood or with the total environment unconsciously. Sometimes, individuals and groups make deliberate and open attempt to stop fighting and start working together. For example, Striking workers stop strike after having an understanding with the management.

3. *It is a Universal Activity*

   Human society is composed of antagonistic elements and hence conflicts are inevitable. No society can function smoothly if the individuals and groups are always engaged in conflict. They must have to make efforts to resolve conflicts, so accommodation is very much necessary. It is found in some degree or other in every society all the time.

4. *It is a Continuous Process*

   Accommodation is not confined to any particular stage or to any fixed social situation. Throughout the life, one has to accommodate oneself with various situations. The continuity of the process of accommodation does not break at all. It is as continuous as man's breathing.

5. *It is a Mixture of both Love and Hatred*

   Accommodation is the combination of two kinds of attitude love and hatred. The attitude of love makes people to cooperate with one another but it is the hate which leads them to create conflicts.

Methods of Accommodation

1. *Admission of One's Defeat*

   This method of accommodation is applicable between the conflicting parties of unequal strength. The stronger group can pressurize the weaker group by its strength. The weaker party submits to the stronger one because of fear of being over-powered.

   For example, in war, the victorious nation imposes its will on the vanquished and the war comes to close when the stronger party achieves a clear-cut victory over the other. The loser has to choose whether it will admit one's own defeat or continue the conflict with the risk of being eliminated together.

2. *Compromise*

   This method is applicable when the combatants are of equal strength. Both the combatants should make some concessions or sacrifices voluntarily for each other because they know that conflict would cause the sheer waste of their energy and resources.

3. *Arbitration and Conciliation*

   Accommodation is also achieved by means of arbitration and conciliation which involves attempt of the third party to resolve conflict between the contending parties. E.g. the conflict between husband and wife, two friends, labor and management are resolved through the intervention of an arbitrator or mediator or conciliator. In conciliation process the conciliator offer only suggestions to terminate a conflict and no binding force upon them. In Arbitration process, the decision of the arbitrator is binding on the concerned parties.

4. *Toleration*

   Toleration is the method of accommodation in which there is no settlement of dispute but there is only the avoidance of overt conflict or open conflict. Toleration is found in the field of religion where different religious groups exists side by side, having different policies and ideologies.

5. *Rationalization*

   Accommodation can be achieved by rationalization. It is a method which involves the withdrawal of contending party from the conflict on the basis of some imaginary explanation to justify his action.

   For example, students believe that their failure in the examination is due to the defects in the evaluation of their answer copy by examiners; they do not see the fact that their preparation for examination is quite inadequate.

6. *Super ordination and Subordination*

   These are the most common method of accommodation which is found in each and every society. In the family the relationships among parents and children are based on this method. E.g. a caste society is a stratified society in which groups have accommodated to a low or high position. When individuals or groups ordinarily accept their relative positions as a matter of fact, accommodation is said to have reached a state of perfection.

Importance of Accommodation

Accommodation is the way which enable people to work together whether they like it or not. Society can hardly go on without accommodation. It not only reduces or controls conflict but also enables the individuals and groups to adjust themselves to changed conditions. It is the basis of social organization and is also essential for social harmony.

4. Assimilation

Assimilation is a fundamental social process by which individuals belonging to different cultures are united into one. It is a slow and gradual process.

According to Biesanz and Biesanz, "Assimilation is the social process whereby individuals or groups come to share the same sentiments and goals".

According to Park and Burgess, "Assimilation is a process of interpenetration and fusion in which individuals and groups acquire the attitudes and values of other persons or groups and by sharing their experience and history, are incorporated with them in a common cultural life".

Characteristics of Assimilation

1. It is an associative process.
2. It is a universal process. It is found in every place and at all times.
3. It is a slow and gradual process because here individual comes to share the expectations of another group and slowly acquires a new set of values.
4. It is an unconscious process because Individuals are not conscious as they discard their own values and acquire new set of values.
5. It is a two-way process and it takes places when groups of individuals borrow cultural phenomenon from each other and incorporates them to their own culture.

The factors affecting assimilation are given as

1. *Toleration*

   Toleration is an important factor which facilitates the process of assimilation. Tolerance helps people to come together, to develop contacts and to participate in common cultural and social activities.

2. *Close Social Contact*

   In Close social contact people promotes the process of assimilation, in which people of different cultures come into close proximity with each other, the assimilation process takes place very easily. The close social contact creates a good understanding among the people and creates a healthy atmosphere in which people exchange their views in a better way.

3. *Amalgamation*

   Amalgamation is another promoting factor of assimilation. By amalgamation, individuals or groups come into close contact to one another. It occurs when two different cultural groups establish matrimonial relationship among themselves. For example, the marital relations among the Hindus and non-Hindus facilitate the process of assimilation. The marital relationship brings the people of different culture very close to one another.

4. *Equal Economic Opportunity*

   The inequality of economic status among the people of different cultural groups hinders the process of assimilation. But the equal economic opportunities facilitate assimilation process. The people having equal economic position have more intimacy that promotes assimilation.

5. *Common Physical Traits*

   Common Physical traits or qualities of the people of different cultures also promote the process of assimilation. The foreign immigrants of the same race can more easily assimilate than those with different races. For example, the Indian who live in America permanently can easily assimilate with the Indian culture.

6. *Cultural Similarity*

   Cultural similarities between two groups of individuals promote assimilation. If there are similarities between culture groups, assimilation take place easily. Similarly, assimilation occurs quickly when two culture groups have common language. Without knowledge of language, the individual remains outside the adopted society. The most important step in assimilation into a new society is, therefore, to lean language.

Factors Hindering Assimilation

There are various factors which hinders assimilation. These factors are given as:

1. *Physical Differences*

   Differences in features, complexion of skin and other physical trait may also help or hinder in assimilation. Generally the adjustment is the easiest for those immigrants whose appearances are most like with the people of the new land.

2. *Cultural Differences*

   Language and religion are usually considered to be main constituents of culture, Immigrants having the same religion and language can easily adjust themselves in other area or country e.g. In America English speaking Protestants are assimilated with the great speed and ease whereas non-Christians who do not speak English, have the greatest difficulty in being assimilated there. Custom and belief are other cultural characteristics that can help or hinder assimilation.

3. *Prejudice*

   Prejudice is a barrier to assimilation. It is the attitude on which segregation depends for its success. Prejudice within a community, within a family or within any group play negative role and creates disunity.

4. *Sense of Superiority and Inferiority*

   Assimilation is hindered by feelings of superiority and inferiority. The people, who have strong feelings of superiority, generally hate the people who suffer from a sense of inferiority. Due to this reason intimate relationship between two groups of people become difficult. Hence, assimilation is retarded.

5. *Domination and Subordination*

   Assimilation between two groups of people is almost impossible where one group dominate the other. The dominant group always considers the people of subordinate group as inferior and exercises its power over them. As a result negative feelings like jealousy, hatred, suspicion and conflict etc. develop among them. All these hinder the process of assimilation.

6. *Isolation*

   Isolation also hinders assimilation. People who live in isolation fail to establish social contacts with others. The isolated people cut off entire social relationship with other people in society. Therefore, the process of assimilation becomes very difficult.

Peer pressure can be reduced by the following:

1. Avoid the situations which make you feel uncomfortable.
2. Get involved in social activities like sports or a social club at college level with others on a positive levels so that your energy can be utilized and you feel lesser peer pressure if you are involved with other teens that possess the same ethics and interests as you do.
3. Use good Humor to get rid of sticky situations and overcome peer pressure.
4. Confide in your parents and teachers they are your first line of defense. It's amazing how you can get rid of tough situation just by telling one of them and you find what's really bugging you.
5. Know your worth-remember you are God's creation and you are created unique with your identity. No two persons are alike, even identical twins are not the same–fingerprints and thoughts. You can just be you. Develop self confidence in yourself.

****

Chapter - 9

Conflict

CONFLICT

Conflict is one of the dissociative or disintegrative social processes. It is a universal and fundamental social process in human relations. It arises only when the attention of the competitors is diverted from the object of competition to themselves. Conflict is anti-thesis of cooperation and also goal oriented.

In simple way we can say it is a process of seeking to obtain rewards by eliminating or weakening the competitors.

According to A.W. Green, "Conflict is the deliberate attempt to oppose, resist or coerce the will of another or others".

According to Gillin and Gillin "Conflict is the social process in which individuals or groups seek their ends by directly challenging the antagonist by violence or threat of violence".

Characteristics

The main characteristics of conflict are as given:

(i) It is a Universal Process

Conflict is an ever-present process. It exists at all places and all times. The cause of the universality of conflict is the increase of man's selfishness and his materialist tendency.

(ii) It is a Personal Activity

Conflict is personal activity and its aim is to eliminate the opposite party. The defeat of the opponent is the main objective in conflict. When competition is personalized it becomes conflict.

(iii) It is Conscious Activity

Conflict is a deliberate attempt to oppose or resist the will of others. It aims at causing loss or injury to persons or groups. So consciously, knowingly or deliberately the parties make struggle with each other in conflict.

(iv) It is an Intermittent Process

There is no continuity in conflict. It is occasionally and it lacks continuity. It may take place all of a sudden and may come to an end after sometime. If the conflict becomes continuous, no society can sustain itself. So it is an intermittent process.

CAUSES OF CONFLICT

Conflict is universal. It cannot be definitely said when conflict came into existence or there is no definite cause for its emergence. According to psychologists, the cause of conflict lies in man's inmate or inborn aggressive tendency or also due to social change. When people does not change along with changes in society, cultural lag occurs which leads to conflict. The old generation and new generation conflict is the result of social change. The rate of change in the moral norms of a society and in man's hopes, demands, and desires is also responsible for the emergence of conflict. For example, the moral norm that children should obey their parents have persisted in our country since time immemorial but now the younger generation wants to go in its own way. In consequence, there is more parent-youth conflict than before.

TYPES OF CONFLICT

There are Two Fundamental Types of Conflict.

1. Direct Conflict

When person or a group injures or destroys the opponent in order to secure a goal or reward, direct conflict occurs; such as litigation, revolution and war.

2. Indirect Conflict

In indirect conflict, attempts are made by individuals or groups to frustrate the efforts of their opponents in an indirect manner. For example, when two manufacturers go on lowering the prices of their commodities till both of them are declared insolvent then indirect conflict take place.

According To George Simmel "Conflict is of three types" which are given as

(i) War

When all the efforts to resolve the conflict between two States fail, war finally breaks out as it is the only alternative to the peaceful means of solution. Although it is dissociative in character yet it has a definitely associative effect.

(ii) Feud

Feud or factional strife does not take place among the states or nations. It usually occurs among the members of the society. This kind of strife is known as intra-group but not the inter-group conflict.

(iii) Litigation

Litigation is a form of conflict which is judicial in nature.

ROLE OF CONFLICT

At the outset, it may be said that conflict causes social disorder, chaos and confusion. It may disrupt social unity but like competition, conflict also performs some positive functions. Conflict is both harmful as well as useful for the society. Role of the conflicts can be further categories into two parts

Positive Role of Conflicts are given as

1. **It promotes the solidarity and fellow-feeling**

   The conflict which promotes the solidarity and fellow-feeling within the groups and societies are known as corporate conflict. This conflict tends to increase the moral and promote the solidarity called in-group threatened by the out-group. For example, in war time cooperation and patriotism among the citizens of a nation are more perfect than in peace time.

2. **It enlarges the victorious group**

   The victorious group either increases its power or incorporates new territory and population. In this way conflict makes possible the emergence of a larger group.

3. **It leads to redefinition of value system**

   Conflict may lead to a redefinition of the situation by the

contesting parties. Generally, the parties which are in conflict with each other give up the old value system and accept new ones when the conflict is over. In this way conflict may give rise to new types of cooperation and accommodation.

4. **It acts as a cementing factor in the establishment of the relation of intimation**

   Conflict in certain cases acts as a cementing factor in the establishment of intimation and friendly relationship among people or parties that were involved in it until a short time ago. For example, the end of the verbal conflict between lovers, friends and married couples leads to the establishment of relations which are now more intimate than before.

The Negative Role of Conflicts is given as

1. **It causes social disorder, chaos and confusion**

   War, a type of conflict, may destroy the lives and properties of which are involved in it. The warring parties generally incur great losses. They gain nothing in comparison with the loss incurred. The modern mode of warfare which can destroy million of people and vast amount of properties within a few minute has brought new fears and anxieties for the mankind.

2. **It disrupts social unity and cohesion**

   Conflict is an anti-thesis to unity and cooperation. It disrupts normal channels of unity. It is a costly way of settling disputes. The results of intergroup conflict are largely negative. Conflict weakens the solidarity of the group by diverting members' attention from group objectives.

3. **It causes a lot of psychological and moral damage**

   The conflict touches the morale of an individual on a personal level. It makes people psychologically weak. It spoils the mental peace of man. It may even make the people to become inhuman. In case, conflict does not come to quick end, it makes the conflicting individuals very weak and apprehensive about losing something.

CONFLICT RESOLUTION METHODS

The conflict resolution method is highly effective to managing conflict and improving their environment.

Which are given as

1. **Collaboration**– This method matches the need of the individuals to build commitment and reach consensus. It can take time and energy and it requires an environment of trust. In this method both sides win.
2. **Compromise**– This method involves some giving and taking on both side; not a perfect outcome but it works if both sides are willing and flexible. Often achieving; Compromise can be done more quickly than collaboration.
3. **Competition**– In this method put one individual's interests ahead of the other. While the conflict might be resolved for a time, the losers do not feel satisfied and the conflict may escalate into different areas. I think this is the riskiest method and it will minimize chances of future cooperation.
4. **Talk to the conflictors**– Two disagreed parties should first try to make an honest effort to discuss matters

constructively keeping an open mind and be willing to listen and to see the conflict from each participant's point of view and explore the facts, issues and possible solutions carefully, so you can resolve conflict effectively.

5. **Mediation**– Try mediation if your effort to resolve the conflicts fails, you may request mediation service through the center for conflict resolution. We will mediate by discussing the problem with both side and by bringing the parties together in a mediation conference. The mediator remains neutral and impartial and helps the parties in finding the best solution.

6. **Arbitration or court**– This method is tried when disputing parties fail to reach a settlement through mediation; they may carry it through arbitration process or the public judicial system. Arbitration is a private adjudicatory process similar to a court law and their decisions are legally binding. The disputants give up the power to create their own solution and place control of their problem in the hand of neutral third party, called an arbitrator. So arbitrator should be the last resort to settle the conflicts.

Conflict Resolution Methods at Work Place

1. **Gather the group**

   As a leader, you need to arrange a meeting with all involved parties to discuss the issue. Give everyone a chance to speak; this is a good opportunity to hear all sides and gain a full understanding of the conflict hence a group meeting may also expedite a resolution that will satisfy everyone.

2. **Be Impartial**

   Don't take side, being a leader you shouldn't display any sort of opinion that favour one person over another. If you are partial towards one person, try to access the situation from all sides to come up with a fair and reasonable solution.

3. **Do not postpone conflict resolution**

   Address the conflict immediately, otherwise the situation could escalate and affect employee performance. Just makes sure not to address the situation too quickly or without careful consideration, as your decision will directly affect others.

General Steps applied to resolve the conflicts

1. Set up a meeting between the conflicting parties to discuss the issue.
2. During conflict resolution, they need to focuses on the problem, not the person.
3. Ask them to listen carefully to one another' point of view, so that everyone feels heard.
4. Be clear about the facts and then work together to agree on a resolution.
5. Get practice by focusing on a mild conflict first and then try it on more significant one.

****

Chapter - 10

Yoga and Meditation for Peace and Harmony

It is well known in today's world that among the many popularly known universal ideas which originate from Hinduism or Sanatana Dharma, Yoga and Meditation are foremost. Millions of people around the world are in to Yoga in some form or the other. Therefore, it is important that we should not only have a good knowledge of Yoga but also practice it.

MEANING OF YOGA

Yoga is an essential practice that helps human beings for development in physical, mental and spiritual domains that brings fulfilment in life. Yoga is the restraint of mental operations or processes. It is the disconnection of connection with sufferings. Yoga is balancing of mind and body and is said to be the unification of the web of dualities. It is said to be the union of individual self with universal self.

In the light of various definitions, Yoga can be described in different forms as below. However, these forms are inter-related.

1. Bhakti Yoga (through devotion)
2. Karma Yoga (through self less action)
3. Janana Yoga (through self-enquiry and knowing)

4. Mantra Yoga (through mantra)
5. Naada Yoga (through transcendental sacred variations)
6. Raja Yoga or Ashtanga Yoga (through eight limbs approach)

ORIGIN OF YOGA

Yoga has existed from Vedic times and its importance is described in several scriptures. In Upanishads, Yoga is referred as an essential means to achieve happiness. It is advised: "Treat the self as the person seated in the body as the chariot. Then, treat the intellect as the driver (charioteer), the mind as the reins and the senses as the horses. The one who has control of mind directed by intellect thereby controlling the senses leads the person to the spiritual goal. Otherwise a person's life will be as of a chariot driven by uncontrolled horses."

Also, in the Bhagavadgita which is known as Yoga Shastra i.e. a scripture on Yoga, Lord Krishna emphasises that the goal of everyone should be to achieve yoga, or state of equanimity. He beautifully describes the blissful state of yogi (i.e. one that has achieved yoga).

Maharishi Patanjali has made great contributions in removing impurities in three domains namely though ayurveda in body for good health and achieving pure mind. He has systematically presented a comprehensive process of yoga through Ashtanga yoga.

"The chief aim of Yoga is to experience the inner spiritual world having realized the truths through the knowledge of process of manifestation of self, senses and body and based on one's own full spiritual development by tuning the outward looking self (mind) inwards through the path of the (central naadi channel in the spine).

The process of yoga encompasses all aspects of human life namely physical, psychological and spiritual. Yoga through its eight limbs is highly practical and scientific. It is highly applicable to all human beings encompassing body, mind and soul.

The yoga system refers to 26 principles with 25 referring to a human being and the 26th referring to Ishwara or God Principle. The 25 principles are

1. Purusha (individual soul)
2. Prakriti (primordial matter)
3. Mahat (intellect)
4. Ahankara (ego-identity)
5. Manas (mind)

   (6-10) the five sensory organs namely ears, skin, eyes, tongue and nose,

   (11-15) the five motor organs namely speech, hands, feet, evacuation and reproduction,

   (16-20) the five elements of subtle perception namely sound, touch, colour, taste and odor, and

   (21-25) the five gross elements namely space, air, fire, water and earth.

Hence, these 25 principles describes the three levels of human beings i.e. physical,psychological and spiritual.

Bases of Yoga by Patanjali

The aim of yoga is to achieve purity and clarity of manas (mind), buddhi (intellect) and chitta (consciousness). This removal of impurities allows the individual to realize and remain in original and normal state of uncontaminated joy and bliss.

The five modes of acquiring knowledge according to Patanjali Maharishi are:

1. Pramana (true cognition based on three means of validity namely direct perception,inference and verbal testimony from a trust-worthy person)
2. Viparaya (false cognotion)
3. Vikalpa (merely verbal based cognition)
4. Nidra(through sleep) and
5. Smriti (through memory)

Process of Yoga by Patanjali-ashtanga Yoga

The eight steps of yoga sutras of ashtanga yoga i.e. (eight limbs) are as under:

1. Yama: This contains five steps, which need to be practiced in domains of thought,speech and action.

(a.) Non-Violence (Ahimsa)

(b.) Truthfulness (Satya)

(c.) Non-Covetedness (Asteya)

(d.) Continence (Bramhacharya)

(e.) Non-receiving (Aparigraha)

2. Niyama: This also contains five sub-steps, which need to be practiced in the domains of thought, speech and action.

(a.) Cleanliness (shoucha)

(b.) Contentment (santosh)

(c.) Austerity (tapas)

(d.) Scriptural study (svaadhyaya)

(e.) Surrender to God (ishvara pranidhanna)

3. **Asanas (Postures):** In Asanas, the body is held steady in postures and movements of body parts are controlled.

4. **Praanayama (Regulation of Vital Force)**: In Praanayama, control of vital forces is focused through proper regulation of breathing exercises.

5. **Pratyaahara:** In this yoga the person practices withdrawing the mind from senses and multiplicity of thoughts. The withdrawn mind is then directed towards the inner-self.

6. **Dhaarana:** It is the development of the ability of the indrawn mind to focus and concentrate on a sacred object (such as vision of guru, chosen diety and other sacred forms).

7. **Dhyaana:** It is referred as meditation, is continous contemplation or concentration on the sacred object.

   Samadhi: It refers to an experience of transcendental state of balance and deep spiritual absorption. It is an individual internalised experiences.

BREATHING EXERCISES IN YOGA

The breath is also a useful tool for meditation. By bringing awareness to your breath, by actually sitting in physical stillness and taking the time to simply listen to it, you can quiet the mind. Most of your thinking is simply illusions the mind creates to distract you from reality. When you calm the mind, you open your awareness to the direct experience of the present. It is at that moment that you discover your true nature and the nature of the world around you.

The breathing exercises are to utilise the three anatomical parts of your lungs. Because of poor posture and bad habits arising from unconscious carelessness, many of you breathe shallowly or with compressed lungs, depriving your body of essential oxygen. Furthermore, insufficient exhalation poisons the body by building up carbon dioxide in your system.

When you become aware of your breathing and recognise that it is the way in which you can control the energy of your body and mind, you can begin to use it. Without proper breathing, hatha yoga is simply a physical exercise. When you start to move with the breath, we experience a change in your state of mind. You become relaxed, focused, and peaceful. You also begin to enjoy our bodies.

With mindfulness and concentration, you can send the energy of the breath throughout the body, releasing tensions, supplying strength, and bringing stillness to areas where you are troubled. When practicing yoga, you often discover parts of your body that are tight, sore, numb, or painful of which you were not even aware. This is the process of developing mindfulness

Relaxation Techniques

Relaxation techniques start by taking your consciousness away from emotionally charged thoughts and directing it to activities that are emotionally neutral such as breath and body awareness. If your attention is on your big toe it is difficult to stay angry, the same is true if you are focussed on the movement of air in and out of the body. Tension will be released with the implementation of conscious deep breathing and the rotation of awareness through various muscles and parts of the body.

The Full Body or Yogic Breath

The yogic breath allows the body to release tension by slowing down the breathing rate, utilising increased air and pranic (energy) capacity and engaging the parasympathetic nervous system (rest and repair). Alternatively, with shallow and quick breathing the sympathetic nervous system activates the "flight and fight" response in which adrenalin and cortisone fill the physical body, a caustic element to cellular health and overall well-being.

For the most part people have very shallow breathing that originates in the upper regions of the torso – effectively the shoulder area. These muscles often give great problems as tension is being held in these areas, especially with work at a computer or desk and even driving will be exacerbate this tension. Shallow breathing increases the work load and will over use those muscles which attach to the rib cage and facilitate the mechanics of breathing.

PROCESS OF YOGIC BREATHING

With the ever-increasing incidence of lifestyle diseases are also increasing like cardio-vascular and nervous system disorders and many more. It is the time for you to address yourselves without external dependence. Your natural breathing technique would not only help in preventing these problems but also help in the "reversal" of several such harmful conditions.

Surprising as it is, almost none of you use the full capacity of your respiratory organs. This is aggravated by our sedentary lifestyles and leads to several complications popularly called- lifestyle disorders. You can alter your natural breathing process by reprogramming your our involuntary system to adopt a new way of breathing.

This breathing technique is called the "Full Yogic breath" or simply Yoga breathing.

First, lie down on your back, relaxed, with hands and legs outstretched and eyes looking up towards the sky. Gently close your eyes and relax.

Step 1: Abdominal breathing

Observe your natural breath. You will notice that as you inhale the abdomen rises and then falls with exhalation. Watch this for a few moments to check this flow. Now begin to deepen, lengthen and extend that movement. That is, while inhaling, let the abdomen rise to its limit and at exhalation let it fall completely. Keep the chest still during this entire process – only move the abdomen. Continue this for 20 breaths and then rest.

Step 2: Thoracic (chest) breathing

Again observe your normal breath, this time focusing your attention on the chest. You will notice the chest moving slightly up at inhalation and down with exhalation. Again observe this pattern for a few moments. Now again, begin to deepen, lengthen and extend that movement. This time, on inhalation expand and lift the rib cage, filling the lungs completely. Then on exhalation, let the lungs collapse fully, sinking to the limits. In this step, keep the abdomen still, moving only the chest. Do this for 20 breath cycles and then stop.

Step 3: Upper chest/shoulder breathing

Focussing on your upper chest, lift and rise into the upper chest and shoulders on the inhalation and relax fully on the exhalation. Again practise for 20 breath cycles.

Step 4: Full Yogic breathing

This combines the above 3 steps in the following way:

First inhale by filling the abdomen and then CONTINUE inhaling as you expand and fill the chest, followed by the upper chest and shoulders. Then exhale first from the abdomen, then the chest, then the upper chest/shoulders. This is one round of the full yogic breath. Repeat this for 20 rounds.

Remember the pattern… Inhaling – abdomen then chest then upper chest/shoulders; Exhaling – abdomen then chest then upper chest/shoulders.

All of the above steps should be done WITHOUT strain. The natural tendency is to heave with effort. The right way is to make it smooth and effortless. Go slow and easy.

Initially you will experience unevenness or bumps in this breathing process – as if there are 4 separate parts to the full yogic breath. This is natural considering the years we have spent breathing improperly.

Instead, try to picture this breath as a continuous wave like pattern – as if the breath moves up from the navel to the throat with every inhalation and then, down from the throat to the navel with each exhalation. It may take a few weeks of practice to perfect a SMOOTH flowing pattern with MINIMUM effort and with MAXIMUM capacity.

Benefits of Yogic Breath

The full yogic breath is the basic building block of the powerful yoga breathing techniques, also called "Pranayama" in Sanskrit, which is known for their multifarious benefits.

Benefits of the full yogic breath are that it

- Releases acute and chronic muscular tensions around the heart and digestive organs.
- Helps sufferers of respiratory illnesses such as asthma and emphysema to overcome the fear of shortness of breath. It actually increases lung capacity.
- Encourages proper nervous stimulus to the cardio-vascular system
- Dramatically reduces emotional and nervous anxiety
- Improves detoxification through increased exchange of carbon dioxide and oxygen
- Amplifies the auto immune system by increased distribution of energy to the endocrine system
- Calms the mind and integrates the mental/physical balance.
- And the real icing is that it contributes to both vitality and relaxation through this single practice.

MEDITATION

Meaning of Meditation

Meditation is a word that has originated from the word *meditates* which mean thinking or contemplating. However meditation (dhyana) is not this.

Actually it is a technique for resting the mind and attaining a state of consciousness that is totally different from the normal waking state. Meditation is not a part of any religion; it is a science, which follows a particular order, has definite principles, and produces results that can be verified.

In meditation, the mind is clear, relaxed, and inwardly focused. When you meditate, you are fully awake and alert, but your mind is not focused on the external world. Meditation requires an inner state that is still and pin-pointed so that the mind becomes silent. When the mind is silent meditation deepens.

It is true that the whole of the body is in the mind, but the whole of the mind is not in the body. Except for the practice of meditation, there is no method to develop control over the totality of the mind.

The goal of meditation is to go beyond the mind and experience our essential nature—which is described as peace, happiness and bliss. But as we tried to meditate, the mind itself is the biggest obstacle standing between ourselves and this awareness. The mind is undisciplined and uncontrolled and it resists any attempts to discipline it or to guide it on a particular path. The mind has a mind of its own. That is why many people sit for meditation and experience only fantasies, daydreams.

When we learn to do this through meditation, we attain the highest of all joys that can ever be experienced by a human being. All the other joys in the world are momentary, but the joy of meditation is immense and everlasting.

So meditation is a practical method for calming yourself and it is a way of training the mind so that you are not distracted and caught up in its endless churning. Meditation teaches you to systematically explore your inner dimensions. It is a system of commitment, not commandment. You are committing to yourself, to your path, and to the goal of knowing yourself.

Definitions of Meditation:

1. Meditation is a practice of concentrated or focus upon a sound, object, visualization, the breath, movement, or attention itself in order to increase awareness of the present moment, reduce stress, promote relaxation, and enhance personal and spiritual growth. Meditation is an intentional and self-regulated focusing of attention, whose purpose is to relax and calm the mind and body.
2. Meditation is a state of consciousness in which the individual eliminates environmental stimuli from awareness so that the mind has a single focus, producing a state of relaxation and relief from stress.
3. Meditation is a technique in which people empties his mind of extraneous thought, with the intent of elevating the mind to a different level and excel in everyday life.
4. Meditation is directing one's attention toward a symbol, sound, thought, or breath to alter the state of consciousness to attain a state of relaxation and stress relief; used for spiritual growth, healing, deepening concentration and unlocking creativity.

Origin of Meditation

Meditation techniques have been practiced for millennia. They were intended to develop spiritual understanding, awareness, and direct experience of ultimate reality. These include the contemplative practices of Christian religious orders, the Buddhist practice of sitting meditation.

Although mediation is an important spiritual practice in many religious and spiritual traditions, it can be practiced by their religious or cultural release of stress and pain stress and pain.

As Western medical practitioners begin to understand the mind's role in health and disease, there has been more interest in the use of meditation in medicine. In hospitals meditative practices are used as a tool for improving health and also used as the primary therapy for treating certain diseases and improving the quality of life of people with debilitating, chronic, or terminal illnesses.

Depending on the type of meditation, the meditators may be concentrating on the sensation of the movement of the breath, counting the breath, silently repeating a sound, chanting, visualizing an image, focusing awareness on the center of the body, opening to all sensory experiences including thoughts, or performing stylized ritual movements with the hands.

Purpose of Meditation

Meditation benefits people with or without acute medical illness or stress. People who meditate regularly have been shown to feel less anxiety and depression. They also report that they experience more enjoyment and appreciation of life and their relationships with others are improved. Meditation produces a state of deep relaxation and a sense of balance. Meditation facilitates a greater sense of calmness, empathy, and acceptance of self and others. Meditation is an important complementary therapy for both the treatment and prevention of many stress related conditions. Regular meditation can reduce the number of symptoms of the illness and disorders experienced by patients.

So Meditation can lead to better health, higher quality of life, and lowered health care costs.

Type of Meditation

Generally meditation is of two types

1. Concentration meditation
2. Mindfulness meditation.

1. Concentration Meditation

It involves focusing attention on a single object. Objects of meditation can include the breath, an inner or external image, a movement pattern or sound, word, or phrase that is repeated silently (mantra). The purpose of concentrative practices is to learn to focus one's attention or develop concentration. When thoughts or emotions arise, the meditator gently directs the mind back to the original object of concentration.

2. Mindfulness Meditation

Mindfulness meditation comes out of traditional Buddhist meditation practices. It involves becoming aware of all thoughts, breathings, feelings, perceptions or sensations as they arise in each moment. In it the meditator sits with closed eyes, focusing the attention on the sensations and movement of the breath for approximately 45-60 minutes at a time, at least once a day. It involves bringing awareness to every activity in daily life. Wandering thoughts or distracting feelings are simply noticed without resisting or reacting to them. The essence of mindfulness meditation is not what one focuses on but rather the quality of awareness the meditator brings to each moment. The goal of mindfulness is for you to be more aware, more in touch with life and whatever is happening in your own body and mind at the time it is happening– that is, the present moment."

On the basis of application it is of two types

1. Transcendental Meditation
2. Relaxation Meditation

1. Transcendental Meditation

TM has its origins in the Vedic tradition of India and was introduced to the West by Maharishi Mahesh Yogi. In it, the meditator sits with closed eyes and concentrates on a single word (mantra) for 20 minutes at a time, twice a day. When thoughts or feelings arise, the attention is brought back to the mantra. "During meditation, awaking of mental activity is said to settle down, until even the subtlest thoug ht is transcended and a complet ely unified wholeness of awareness is experienced. In this silent, self-referential state of pure wakefulness, consciousness is fully awake to itself alone…." At the end we can say TM practices are more beneficial than other meditation practices.

2. Relaxation Meditation

Dr. Herbert Benson developed this approach after observing the profound health benefits of a state of bodily calm he calls "the relaxation response." In order to elicit this response in the body, he teaches patients to focus upon the repetition of a word, sound, prayer, phrase, or movement activity (including swimming, jogging, yoga, and even knitting) for 10-20 minutes at a time, twice a day. Patients are also taught not to pay attention to distracting thoughts and to return their focus to the original repetition. The choice of the focused repetition is upto the individual. The meditator can choose what is personally meaningful, such as any prayer or phrase etc.

METHODS OR TECHNIQUES OF MEDITATION

The process of cultivating stillness begins with the body or learning how to be still is the method of meditation which is given as.

It has mainly three steps:

1. Preparation for Meditation
2. Meditation Practice
3. Meditation in everyday life

1. Preparation of Meditation

1. Choose a peaceful environment

Meditation should be practiced in peaceful environment. This will enable you to focus exclusively on the task at hand and avoid bombarding your mind with outside stimuli. Turn off TV sets, the phone or other noisy appliances. In fact, being aware of these noises but not letting them dominate your thoughts is an important component of successful meditation. As long as you don't sit near a busy roadway or another source of loud noise, you can find peace under a tree or sitting upon some lush grass in a favorite corner of the garden.

2. Wear comfortable clothes

Wear comfortable clothes during mediation. It can be difficult if you feel physically uncomfortable due to tight or restrictive clothing. Try to wear loose clothing during meditation practice and make sure to remove your shoes. Take off your shoes and jacket, open the collar of your shirt and remove your belt.

3. ***Decide the duration of mediation***

   Before you begin meditation, you should decide how long you are going to mediate. Many meditators recommend twenty minute sessions twice a day, beginners can start with doing as little as five minutes, once a day. You should also try to meditate at the same time each day – whether it's 15 minutes first in the morning, or five minutes on your lunch hour. Whatever time you choose, try to make mediation at a fixed time of your daily routine.

4. ***Sit in a comfortable position***

   It is very important that you are comfortable while you meditate, meditation is practiced by sitting on a cushion on the ground. You can sit without crossing your legs, on a cushion, chair or a meditation bench. Meditation benches are usually built with a tilted seat. The most important thing is that you are comfortable and relaxed so that your spine supports all of your weight from the waist up. It requires practice to find the position that allows you to relax your whole body only slight effort being used to maintain your balance. Whenever you feel tension, relax the area. If you can't relax it without slumping, check the alignment of your posture and seek to re-balance your body so that area can be relaxed.

5. ***State of eyes***

   Medication can be performed with the eyes open or

closed, however as a beginner it may be best to first try meditating with you closed eyes. This will block out any external visual stimulation and prevent you from becoming distracted as you focus on calming your mind. You can also try practicing with your eyes open. This can be helpful if you are either falling asleep or concentrating too hard with your eyes closed.

2. *Meditation Practices*

1. Follow your breathing– It is most basic and universal of all mediation techniques, breathing meditation is a great place to start your practice. Try to focus on your breathing and only on your breathing, just attempt to know it and be aware of it. Don't worry if your mind starts to wander –you are beginner and becoming good at meditation after practice. Just make an effort to refocus your mind on your breathing and try to think of nothing else.

Before Practicing Meditation you Must Clear your Mind

1. To meditate, you must focus on one thing maximum.
2. If you're a beginner, it might help to focus on one thing, like a mantra or visual object.
3. Concentrate on a simple visual object– You can also concentrate on a simple visual object and allow you to reach a level of deeper consciousness. This is a form of open-eye meditation. The visual object can be anything you wish, though many people find the flame of a candle light. Other possible objects include flowers, pictures or statues of divine beings. Place the object at eye level, so you don't need to strain your head and neck to view it.

Once you are focused entirely on the object, with no other stimuli reaching your brain, you should feel a sense of deep peacefulness.

4. Do a body Scan– Doing a body scan involves focusing on each individual body part and consciously relaxing it. It is a simple meditation technique which allows you to relax the mind as you relax the body.

   First Close your eyes and then start body scanning and pick a starting point on your body, usually the toes. Concentrate on whatever sensations you can feel in your toes, and make a conscious effort to relax any contracted muscles and release any tension or tightness. Once the toes are fully relaxed, move on to your feet and repeat the relaxation process.

   Continue along your body, moving upwards from your feet to your calves, knees, thighs, buttocks, hips, abdomen, chest, back, shoulders, arms, hands, fingers, neck, face, ears and top of your head. Take as long as you want.

   Once you have completed the relaxation of each individual body part, focus on your body as a whole and enjoy the sensation of calmness and looseness you have achieved. Focus on your breathing for several minutes before coming out of your mediation practice.

5. Try Heart Chakra Meditation– The heart chakra is one of seven chakras, or energy centers, located within the body. The heart chakra is located in the center of the chest which is associated with love, compassion, peace and acceptance. This meditation involves getting in touch with these feelings and sending them out into the world.

Feel your body from the inside. You feel the energy field flow in your body. Focusing your attention on that energy field, will not only help you stay in the present but also will help you connect with your being and flow of life in you.

Meditation in Everyday life

1. ***Practice mindfulness meditation in your everyday life–*** You can also practice mindfulness meditation throughout your day to day life. For example, in moments of stress, try to take a few seconds to focus solely on your breathing and empty your mind of any negative thoughts or emotions. You can also practice mindfulness meditation while you eat, becoming aware of the food and of the sensations you experience as you eat. This is called mindfully living.
2. ***Follow a healthy life style–*** A healthy lifestyle can contribute to more effective and beneficial meditation, so try to eat healthily, exercise and get enough sleep. You should also avoid watching too much television or drinking or smoking before meditation, as these activities can make the mind unsensitive and prevent you from achieving the level of concentration that is necessary for successful meditation.
3. ***Reading spiritual books–*** Read spiritual books and sacred writings can help you to understand meditation and inspire them to strive for inner peace and spiritual understanding.
4. Take a guided meditation classes– If you are unsure to meditating at home, you may take a guided meditation class with an experienced teacher first.

5. ***Meditation at same time everyday***– It is important that you make an effort to do your meditation practice at the same time every day. In this way, the meditation will quickly become a part of your everyday life and you will feel its benefits much more profoundly. Early in the morning is a good time to meditate, before your mind becomes consumed with the stressed and worries of the day.
6. ***Understand that meditation is a journey***– The purpose of meditation is to calm the mind, achieve inner peace and reach a higher spiritual dimension. So we can say meditation is a journey, where every step along the path of enlightenment brings you closer to the peak of peace and calmness. As long as you feel calmer, happier and more at peace at the end of your practice, you will know that your meditation was successful.

Precautions

Meditation appears to be safe for most people. There are some case and studies noting some adverse effects. Thirty-three to 50% of the people participating in long silent meditation retreats (two weeks to three months) reported increased tension, anxiety, confusion, and depression. On the other hand, some people also reported very positive effects from their meditation practice. According to Psychologist meditation may not be recommended for people with psychotic disorders, severe depression, and other severe personality disorders unless they are also receiving psychological or medical treatment.

Side Effects

There are no reported side effects of meditation except for positive benefits.

BENEFITS OF MEDITATION

Meditation for Self and Inner Expansion

In ancient times, meditation was used for enlightenment and to find the self.

- Meditation is a way to get rid of misery, to overcome challenges posed by life.
- Meditation has been the way to improve one's abilities—physical as well as mental.
- The more responsibility you have in life, more is the need of meditation.
- It helps in developing greater intuitive capability.
- It helps in developing Concentration

Meditate for Physical and Mental Health

- Meditation brings better health to us.
- Meditation is food for soul.
- It is an energizer for mind.
- It is better for physical and mental health.

Meditation for Happiness

- Meditation helps to change your perception, perspective.
- It helps you in your relationship with people around,

you know how you interact with people, what you see, what you say and how you act or react in different situations.

- So, in general, it helps in creating a violence-free society, disease-free body, confusion-free state of mind, inhibition-free intellect, trauma-free memory and sorrow-free soul.

****

REFERENCES

1. Aldine Transaction Baumeister, R. F. (Ed) (1999) The Self in Social Psychology Philadelphia, PA: Psychology Press (Taylor & Francis).
2. Argyle, M. (2008). Social Encounters: Contributions to social interaction.
3. B. S. Goel (1988): Psychology-Analysis and Meditation, Third Eye Foundation of India, Sonipat, Haryana.
4. Bee, H. L. (1992). The developing child. London. Harpercollins.
5. C. R. Snyder, (2011) Positive Psychology: The Scientific And Practical exploration of Human Sage Publication.
6. Canevello, A. Croker A. Croker J. Interpersnoal goals, other regard for the self and self esteen. The paradoxial consequences of self image and compasionate goals. Eeer, J. Soc. Piychol. 2011:41[4] : 422-434 Accessed vialilt.il
7. Developing Soft Skills by Robert M. Sherfield, Rhonda J., Patricia J. Moodi; Cornerstone Publications.
8. Dr. Kiruba Charles & V. Arul (2015): Peace and Value Education, Selv.
9. Dr. Rupashree kubalker (2015): Know Your Stress-Manage Your Stress, Neel Kamal Publishers.
10. Effective Business Communication by Murphy; The McGraw Hill Company, 7th Edition.
11. Frcudian Psychoanalytic Theory of Personality, Boundless Psychology, Boundless, 6 September 2015

12. Gardner, Cavin S. Hall, Richard F. Thompson (1975): Psychology Worth Publishers Inc.

13. Gary S. Topichik (2008): Managing Workplace Negativity, PHI, Delhi.

14. H. K. Kaul (2013): Yoga Asana for Everyone, Surjeet Publisher.

15. Hans, T. (2000): A meta-analysis of the effects of adventure programming on locus of control. Journal of Contemporary Psychotherapy, 30 (1), 33-60.

16. Hattie J. A., Marsh H. W., Neill J. T. & Richards G. E. (1997). Adventure Education and Outward Bound: Out-of-class experiences that have a lasting effect. Review of Educational Research, 67, 43-87.

17. J. A. Hadfield (1983): Psychology and Morals, Methuen & Co. London.

18. Kuhn M. H. (1960): Self attitudes by age,sex and professional training. Sociological Quarterly, 1, 39-56.

19. Lewis M. (1990): Self-Knowledge and social development in early life. In L. A. Pervin (Ed.), Handbook of personality (pp.277-300). New York: Guilford.

20. Nanette E. Tummers: (2009) Teaching yoga for life.

21. NCERT (2005): Draft, curriculum framework (2005).

22. Nemours Foundation, KidHealth.org. Teens Health: Body Image & Self Esteen; A Self – Help Guide Accessed 11/ 5/ 2013.

23. Pachauri D & Nand V. K., Fundamental of Educational Technology (2007).

24. Robert. S. Feldonan (2009): Essentials of Understanding Psychology Seventh Edition, Tata McGraw Hill, New Delhi.

25. Sheorron Bienvenu (2008): The Presentation Skills Workshop, Prentice Hall of India, New Delhi

26. Sherrill H.K, (2010): Psychology: PH1 Learning Private Limited.

27. Steve Duck, (2012): The Basic of Communication: A relation Perspective Sage Publishers.

28. Substance Abuse and Mental Services Adminiehation, Building Self Esteen: A Self Help Guide Accessed 11/ 5 / 2013

29. www.softskills.com

30. www.softskillsindia.com

31. www.softskillsworld.com

****

